Kaplan Publishing are constantly finding new ways to make a difference to your studies and our exciting online resources really do offer something different to students looking for exam success.

This book comes with free MyKaplan online resources so that you can study anytime, anywhere. **This free online resource is not sold separately and is included in the price of the book.**

Having purchased this book, you have access to the following online study materials:

CONTENT	AAT	
	Text	Kit
Electronic version of the book	✓	✓
Progress tests with instant answers	✓	
Mock assessments online	✓	✓
Material updates	✓	✓

D0294253

How to access your online resources

Kaplan Financial students will already have a MyKaplan account and these extra resources will be available to you online. You do not need to register again, as this process was completed when you enrolled. If you are having problems accessing online materials, please ask your course administrator.

If you are not studying with Kaplan and did not purchase your book via a Kaplan website, to unlock your extra online resources please go to www.mykaplan.co.uk/addabook (even if you have set up an account and registered books previously). You will then need to enter the ISBN number (on the title page and back cover) and the unique pass key number contained in the scratch panel below to gain access. You will also be required to enter additional information during this process to set up or confirm your account details.

If you purchased through Kaplan Flexible Learning or via the Kaplan Publishing website you will automatically receive an e-mail invitation to MyKaplan. Please register your details using this email to gain access to your content. If you do not receive the e-mail or book content, please contact Kaplan Publishing.

Your Code and Information

This code can only be used once for the registration of one book online. This registration and your online content will expire when the final sittings for the examinations covered by this book have taken place. Please allow one hour from the time you submit your book details for us to process your request.

Please scratch the film to access your MyKaplan code.

Please be aware that this code is case-sensitive and you will need to include the dashes within the passcode, but not when entering the ISBN. For further technical support, please visit www.MyKaplan.co.uk

AAT

AQ2016

Elements of Costing

EXAM KIT

This Exam Kit supports study for the following AAT qualifications:
AAT Foundation Certificate in Accounting – Level 2
AAT Foundation Diploma in Accounting and Business – Level 2
AAT Foundation Certificate in Bookkeeping – Level 2
AAT Foundation Award in Accounting Software – Level 2
AAT Level 2 Award in Accounting Skills to Run Your Business
AAT Foundation Certificate in Accounting at SCQF Level 5

British Library Cataloguing-in-Publication Data

A catalogue record for this book is available from the British Library.

Published by:

Kaplan Publishing UK

Unit 2 The Business Centre

Molly Millar's Lane

Wokingham

Berkshire

RG41 2QZ

ISBN: 978-1-78740-281-2

© Kaplan Financial Limited, 2018

Printed and bound in Great Britain.

CONTENTS

Features in this exam kit

In addition to providing a wide ranging bank of real exam style questions, we have also included in this kit:

- unit-specific information and advice on exam technique

- our recommended approach to make your revision for this particular unit as effective as possible.

You will find a wealth of other resources to help you with your studies on the AAT website:

www.aat.org.uk/

Quality and accuracy are of the utmost importance to us so if you spot an error in any of our products, please send an email to mykaplanreporting@kaplan.com with full details, or follow the link to the feedback form in MyKaplan.

Our Quality Co-ordinator will work with our technical team to verify the error and take action to ensure it is corrected in future editions.

UNIT-SPECIFIC INFORMATION

THE EXAM

The assessment will comprise fifteen independent tasks. Students will be assessed by computer-based assessment.

In any one assessment, students may not be assessed on all content, or on the full depth or breadth of a piece of content. The content assessed may change over time to ensure validity of assessment, but all assessment criteria will be tested over time.

The learning outcomes for this unit are as follows:

	Learning outcome	Weighting
1	Understand the cost recording system within an organisation	20%
2	Use cost recording techniques	60%
3	Provide information on actual and budgeted costs and income	20%
	Total	100%

Time allowed

90 minutes

PASS MARK

The pass mark for all AAT CBAs is 70%.

🕐 **Always keep your eye on the clock and make sure you attempt all questions!**

DETAILED SYLLABUS

The detailed syllabus and study guide written by the AAT can be found at:

www.aat.org.uk/

INDEX TO QUESTIONS AND ANSWERS

		Page number	
		Question	Answer

EXAM TECHNIQUE

- **Do not skip any of the material** in the syllabus.

- **Read each question** *very* carefully.

- **Double-check your answer** before committing yourself to it.

- Answer **every** question – if you do not know an answer to a multiple choice question or true/false question, you don't lose anything by guessing. Think carefully before you **guess**.

- If you are answering a multiple-choice question, **eliminate first those answers that you know are wrong.** Then choose the most appropriate answer from those that are left.

- **Don't panic** if you realise you've answered a question incorrectly. Getting one question wrong will not mean the difference between passing and failing.

Computer-based exams – tips

- Do not attempt a CBA until you have **completed all study material** relating to it.

- On the AAT website there is a CBA demonstration. It is **ESSENTIAL** that you attempt this before your real CBA. You will become familiar with how to move around the CBA screens and the way that questions are formatted, increasing your confidence and speed in the actual exam.

- Be sure you understand how to use the **software** before you start the exam. If in doubt, ask the assessment centre staff to explain it to you.

- Questions are **displayed on the screen** and answers are entered using keyboard and mouse. At the end of the exam, you are given a certificate showing the result you have achieved.

- In addition to the traditional multiple-choice question type, CBAs will also contain **other types of questions**, such as number entry questions, drag and drop, true/false, pick lists or drop down menus or hybrids of these.

- In some CBAs you will have to type in complete computations or written answers.

- You need to be sure you **know how to answer questions** of this type before you sit the exam, through practice.

KAPLAN'S RECOMMENDED REVISION APPROACH

QUESTION PRACTICE IS THE KEY TO SUCCESS

Success in professional examinations relies upon you acquiring a firm grasp of the required knowledge at the tuition phase. In order to be able to do the questions, knowledge is essential.

However, the difference between success and failure often hinges on your exam technique on the day and making the most of the revision phase of your studies.

The **Kaplan Study Text** is the starting point, designed to provide the underpinning knowledge to tackle all questions. However, in the revision phase, poring over text books is not the answer.

Kaplan Pocket Notes are designed to help you quickly revise a topic area; however you then need to practise questions. There is a need to progress to exam style questions as soon as possible, and to tie your exam technique and technical knowledge together.

The importance of question practice cannot be over-emphasised.

The recommended approach below is designed by expert tutors in the field, in conjunction with their knowledge of the examiner and the specimen assessment.

You need to practise as many questions as possible in the time you have left.

OUR AIM

Our aim is to get you to the stage where you can attempt exam questions confidently, to time, in a closed book environment, with no supplementary help (i.e. to simulate the real examination experience).

Practising your exam technique is also vitally important for you to assess your progress and identify areas of weakness that may need more attention in the final run up to the examination.

In order to achieve this we recognise that initially you may feel the need to practice some questions with open book help.

Good exam technique is vital.

THE KAPLAN REVISION PLAN

Stage 1: Assess areas of strengths and weaknesses

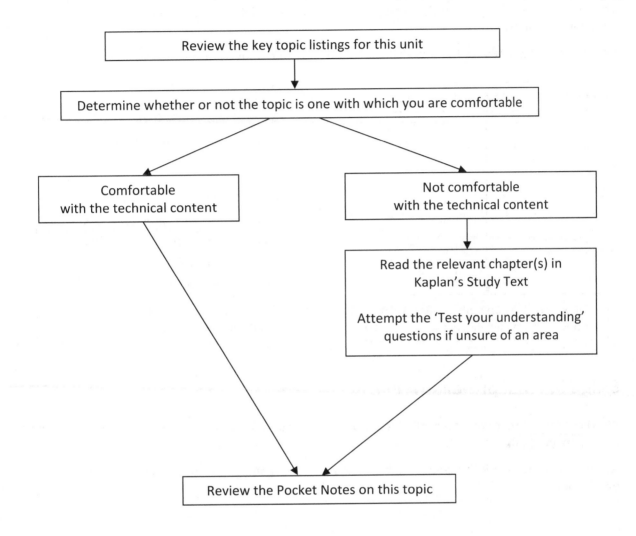

Stage 2: Practice questions

Follow the order of revision of topics as presented in this Kit and attempt the questions in the order suggested.

Try to avoid referring to Study Texts and your notes and the model answer until you have completed your attempt.

Review your attempt with the model answer and assess how much of the answer you achieved.

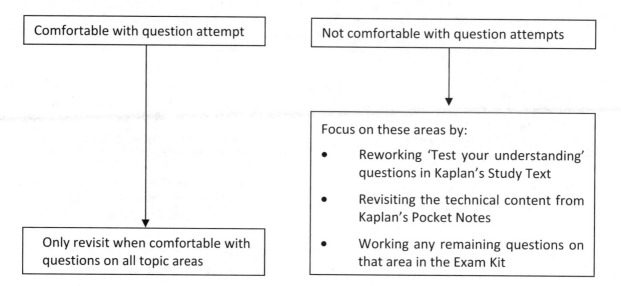

Comfortable with question attempt	Not comfortable with question attempts

Focus on these areas by:

- Reworking 'Test your understanding' questions in Kaplan's Study Text

- Revisiting the technical content from Kaplan's Pocket Notes

- Working any remaining questions on that area in the Exam Kit

Only revisit when comfortable with questions on all topic areas

Stage 3: Final pre-exam revision

We recommend that you **attempt at least one mock examination** containing a set of previously unseen exam-standard questions.

Attempt the mock CBA online in timed, closed book conditions to simulate the real exam experience.

KAPLAN PUBLISHING

Section 1

PRACTICE QUESTIONS

COST CLASSIFICATION

FINANCIAL AND MANAGEMENT ACCOUNTING

1 FAMA

The table below lists some of the characteristics of financial accounting and management accounting systems.

Indicate two characteristics for each system by putting a tick in the relevant column of the table below:

Characteristic	Financial accounting	Management accounting
• Have to be produced annually.		
• Analyses historic events to help produce forecasts.		
• Is always produced using accounting standards.		
• Is produced on an ad hoc basis when required.		

2 FINANCIAL AND MANAGEMENT

The table below lists some of the characteristics of financial accounting and management accounting systems.

Indicate two characteristics for each system by putting a tick in the relevant column of the table below:

Characteristic	Financial accounting	Management accounting
• Must be presented as specified by the Companies Act and accounting standards.		
• Helps managers run the business on a day-to-day basis.		
• Used as the basis for the calculation of the organisation's tax charge.		
• Can include anything that managers feel is useful for the business.		

3   MAFA

The table below lists some of the characteristics of financial accounting and management accounting systems.

Indicate two characteristics for each system by putting a tick in the relevant column of the table below:

Characteristic	Management accounting	Financial accounting
• It is based on past events.		
• Its purpose is to provide information for managers.		
• It is based on future events.		
• It complies with company law and accounting rules.		

4   FEATURES

The table below lists some features typical of financial accounting and management accounting systems.

Indicate which feature applies to which system by putting a tick in the relevant column of the table below:

Feature	Financial accounting	Management accounting
• Analysis of profit by cost centre.		
• Statement of profit or loss using format as dictated by accounting standards and company law.		
• Cash flow forecasts.		
• Cost per unit calculation.		

COST AND PROFIT CENTRES

5   JEREMY

Jeremy operates a business that bakes bread. These are made in a small bakery and then sent to Jeremy's shop, where they are sold. Jeremy also has a small office where all of the administration is undertaken.

Identify whether the following departments are likely to be profit or cost centres by putting a tick in the relevant column of the table below:

Department	Cost centre	Profit centre
• Bakery		
• Shop		✓
• Office	✓	

6   PRINT PLC

Print plc is a large company that prints and sells books. It is split into three divisions – binding, shops and marketing. The binding department prints the books. These are then either transferred to Print's chain of shops where they are sold to the public, or sold direct from the binding department to corporate clients. The marketing department produces all of Print's advertising.

Identify whether the following departments are likely to be profit or cost centres by putting a tick in the relevant column of the table below:

Department	Cost centre	Profit centre
• Binding		
• Shops		✓
• Marketing		

7   HOOCH PLC

Identify whether the following definitions are of be profit, cost, or investment centres by putting a tick in the relevant column of the table below:

Department	Cost centre	Profit centre	Investment centre
• Hooch's manager has no responsibility for income or asset purchases and disposals.	✓		
• Hooch's manager is assessed on the profitability of their department, as well as how effectively they have controlled their assets.			✓
• Hooch's manager is responsible for income and expenditure of their department only.	✓		

CLASSIFYING COSTS BY ELEMENT (MATERIALS, LABOUR OR OVERHEADS)

8   VVV LTD

VVV Ltd manufactures toy planes.

Classify the following costs by element (materials, labour or overheads) by putting a tick in the relevant column of the table below:

Cost	Materials	Labour	Overheads
• Paint used on the planes.	✓		
• Depreciation of the machines used in the factory.			✓
• Oil used on the machines in the factory.			✓
• Salary of worker assembling the planes.		✓	

9 TRIP LTD

Trip Ltd is a company that provides travel insurance.

Classify the following costs by element (materials, labour or overheads) by putting a tick in the relevant column of the table below:

Cost	Materials	Labour	Overheads
• Wages of the insurance clerks dealing with claims.		✓	
• Rent of the office.			
• Paper used to print off insurance policies.			
• Salary of the office manager.			✓

10 FRUWT LTD

FRUWT Ltd manufactures and sells fruit juice.

Classify the following costs by element (materials, labour or overheads) by putting a tick in the relevant column of the table below:

Cost	Materials	Labour	Overheads
• Purchase of fruit for juicing.	✓		
• Electricity used by juicing machines.			
• Water added to the juice before sale.			
• Wages of staff operating juicing machinery.			

11 MARTIN

Martin provides legal services in his home town.

Classify the following costs by element (materials, labour or overheads) by putting a tick in the relevant column of the table below:

Cost	Materials	Labour	Overheads
• Stationery used in Martin's court cases.	✓		
• Wages of Martin's secretary.			
• Water rates for Martin's office.			
• Cost of training courses taken by Martin.			✓

CLASSIFYING COSTS BY NATURE (DIRECT OR INDIRECT)

12 RUSSELL

Russell runs a newspaper.

Classify the following costs by nature (direct or indirect) by putting a tick in the relevant column of the table below:

Cost	Direct	Indirect
• Paper used in the newspapers.		
• Wages of warehouse staff.		
• Heat and light for head office.		
• Ink used in printing the newspapers.		

13 RUSSETT LTD

Russett Ltd is in business as a tablet computer manufacturer.

Classify the following costs by nature (direct or indirect) by putting a tick in the relevant column of the table below:

Cost	Direct	Indirect
• Glass used to make tablets.		
• Insurance of factory.		
• Wages of workers assembling tablets.		
• Cost of entertaining corporate clients.		

14 SCOTLAND LTD

Scotland Ltd makes sports clothing.

Classify the following costs by nature (direct or indirect) by putting a tick in the relevant column of the table below:

Cost	Direct	Indirect
• Cleaners' wages.		
• Advertising expense.		
• Material used in production.		
• Production manager's wages.		
• Machinist wages.		

15 DIRECT OR INDIRECT

Classify the following costs by nature (direct or indirect) by putting a tick in the relevant column of the table below:

Cost	Direct	Indirect
• Chargeable hour for a lawyer.		
• Machine hire for a building contractor in a long term contract.		
• Electricity for a garden centre.		
• Audit fee for a restaurant.		

16 DIRECT COSTS

Direct costs are conventionally deemed to:

A   be constant in total when activity levels alter

B   be constant per unit of activity

C   vary per unit of activity where activity levels alter

D   vary in total when activity levels remain constant

CLASSIFYING COSTS BY FUNCTION (PRODUCTION, ADMINISTRATION OR SELLING AND DISTRIBUTION)

17 NOOGLE LTD

Noogle Ltd produces microwaveable ready meals.

Classify the following costs by function (production, administration, or selling and distribution) by putting a tick in the relevant column of the table below:

Cost	Production	Administration	Selling and distribution
• Purchases of plastic for ready meal containers.			
• Depreciation of sales department's delivery lorries.			
• Insurance of office computers.			
• Salaries of production workers.			

18   HEAVING LTD

Heaving Ltd produces exercise equipment.

Classify the following costs by function (production, administration, or selling and distribution) by putting a tick in the relevant column of the table below:

Cost	Production	Administration	Selling and distribution
• Paper used to print off sales invoices.			
• Metal used to make weights and bars.			
• Depreciation of sales person's vehicle.			
• Repairs to machine in factory.			

19   KORMA PLC

Classify the following costs by function (production, administration, selling and distribution or finance) by putting a tick in the relevant column of the table below:

Cost	Production	Administration	Selling and distribution	Finance
• Direct materials.				
• Sales director salary.				
• Head office printer ink.				
• Direct labour.				
• Bank charges.				

20   JAMES

James makes false teeth.

Classify the following costs by function (production, administration, selling and distribution or finance) by putting a tick in the relevant column of the table below:

Cost	Production	Administration	Selling and distribution	Finance
• Salary of receptionist.				
• Plastic used in false teeth.				
• Stationery provided to all departments.				
• Interest on James' bank overdraft.				
• Electricity for James' factory.				

CLASSIFYING COSTS BY BEHAVIOUR (FIXED, VARIABLE OR SEMI-VARIABLE)

21 QUARK LTD

Quark Ltd runs a bar.

Classify the following costs by their behaviour (fixed, variable, or semi-variable) by putting a tick in the relevant column of the table below:

Cost	Fixed	Variable	Semi-variable
• Bar manager's salary.	✓		
• Alcohol used to make drinks.			
• Rent of bar.	✓		
• Telephone costs, including standard line rental charge.			

22 MORN LTD

Morn Ltd is a manufacturer of chairs and stools.

Classify the following costs by their behaviour (fixed, variable, or semi-variable) by putting a tick in the relevant column of the table below:

Cost	Fixed	Variable	Semi-variable
• Wood used in production.		✓	
• Advertising manager's salary.			
• Electricity costs which include a standing charge.			✓
• Labour costs paid on a piecework basis.	✓	✓	

23 STEPPED FIXED COST

Which of the following would usually be classed as a stepped fixed cost?

A   Supervisor's wages

B   Raw materials

C   Rates

D   Telephone

24 BRAETAK LTD

Classify the following costs by their behaviour (fixed, variable, or semi-variable) by putting a tick in the relevant column of the table below:

Cost	Fixed	Variable	Semi-variable
• Rent of an office building.			
• Wages of production staff paid on an hourly basis.			
• Wages of production staff paid by a piece rate method.			
• Sales staff paid a basic wage plus commission for each unit sold.			

25 ODO LTD

Odo Ltd is a manufacturer of clothes.

Classify the following costs by their behaviour (fixed, variable, or semi-variable) by putting a tick in the relevant column of the table below:

Cost	Fixed	Variable	Semi-variable
• Material used in the production process.			
• Safety review fee for the year.			
• Electricity costs which include a standing charge.			
• Labour costs paid on a per unit basis.			

26 DEFINITIONS

Identify the following costs by their behaviour (fixed, variable, or semi-variable) by putting a tick in the relevant column of the table below:

Behaviour	Fixed	Variable	Semi-variable	Stepped cost
• This type of cost increases in direct proportion to the amount of units produced.				
• This type of cost has a fixed and a variable element.			✓	
• This type of cost remains constant despite changes in output.				
• This type of cost is fixed within a certain range of output.				✓

27   MATCH A GRAPH

Match a graph to each of the following costs by labelling each graph with a letter (A–E):

(a)   Variable cost per unit

(b)   Total fixed cost

(c)   Stepped fixed costs

(d)   Total variable cost

(e)   Semi-variable cost

Note: Each graph may relate to more than one cost.

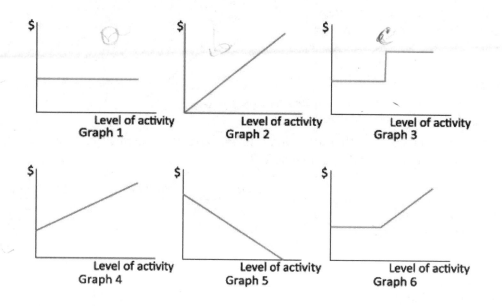

COST CODING

28   BYTES LTD

Bytes Limited operates an IT consultancy business and uses a coding system for its elements of cost (materials, labour or overheads) and then further classifies each element by nature (direct or indirect cost) as below:

So, for example, the code for direct materials is A100.

Element of cost	Code	Nature of cost	Code
Materials	A	Direct	100
		Indirect	200
Labour	B	Direct	100
		Indirect	200
Overheads	C	Direct	100
		Indirect	200

Code the following costs, extracted from invoices and payroll, using the table below:

Cost	Code
• Salary of trainee IT consultant.	
• Planning costs to renew lease of the office.	
• Wages of the office manager.	
• Cleaning materials used by cleaner.	

29 HERO LTD

Hero Ltd, a manufacturer of superhero costumes, uses a numerical coding structure based on one profit centre and three cost centres as outlined below. Each code has a sub-code so each transaction will be coded as ***/***

Profit/cost centre	Code	Sub-classification	Sub-code
Sales	115	Women's costumes	085
		Men's costumes	095
Production	225	Direct cost	110
		Indirect cost	115
Administration	485	Direct cost	220
		Indirect cost	230
Selling and distribution	760	Direct cost	320
		Indirect cost	340

Code the following revenue and expense transactions, which have been extracted from purchase invoices, sales invoices and payroll, using the table below:

Transaction	Code
• Cost of major advertising campaign.	
• Oil for machinery in factory.	
• Silk used in manufacturing of costumes.	
• Insurance of head office.	
• Sale of women's costumes to a supermarket chain.	
• Wages paid to delivery van drivers.	

30   VILLAIN LTD

Villain Ltd, a mining company, uses a numerical coding structure based on one profit centre and three cost centres as outlined below. Each code has a sub-code so each transaction will be coded as ***/***

Profit/cost centre	Code	Sub-classification	Sub-code
Revenue	011	Gold sales	100
		Other sales	200
Production	015	Direct Cost	100
		Indirect Cost	200
Administration	019	Direct Cost	100
		Indirect Cost	200
Selling and distribution	024	Direct Cost	100
		Indirect Cost	200

Code the following revenue and expense transactions, which have been extracted from purchase invoices, sales invoices and payroll, using the table below:

Transaction	Code
• Petrol used to run drilling machinery.	
• Sale of silver to a jewellery manufacturer.	
• Replacement of worn out drilling machinery parts.	
• Depreciation of fleet of delivery lorries.	
• Salary of finance director.	
• Sale of gold to an electronics company.	

31   NAYULZ LTD

Nayulz Limited operates a chain of nail salons across Europe and America.

Code the following transactions for the project, using the table below. Each transaction should have a five-character code.

Activity	Code	Nature of cost	Sub-code
Investments	IN	External	100
		Internal	110
Revenues	RE	Europe	225
		America	228
Costs	CO	Material	315
		Labour	318
		Overheads	325

Code the following costs, extracted from invoices and payroll, using the table below:

Cost	Code
• Income earned from salons in New York City, America.	2
• Bank loans raised to open a new store in London.	
• Nail polish purchased for use in salon.	
• Heat and light for salon.	
• Nayulz funds invested in new project.	

32 JUMPER LTD

Jumper Ltd manufactures a range of different items of clothing, which it sells to various types of organisation.

The company analyses sales using an alphanumeric coding system depending on the type of clothing being sold, as well as the type of organisation the clothes are being sold to.

Type of clothing	Code
Trousers	TRS
Jumpers	KNI
Coats	MCN

Sale made to:	Code
Individuals	315
Shops	425
Offices	515
Factories	635

For example, sale of coats to a factory would be coded as MCN/635

Code the following transactions, using the table below:

Sale	Code
• Sale of one jumper to Mrs S. Wooley.	KNI
• Sale of protective trousers to a factory in London.	
• Sale of large coats to an office in Birmingham.	MCN
• Sale of woolen jumpers to a shop in Halifax.	KNI
• Sale of four coats to Mr A. West.	MCN 315
• Sale of three hundred trousers to a shop in Manchester.	TRS 425

33   GREENFINGERS

Greenfingers Ltd runs a garden centre and uses a coding system for its transactions.

Code the following transactions, using the table below. Each transaction must have a five character code.

Element of cost	Code	Nature of cost	Code
Investments	IN	External	515
		Internal	615
Revenues	RV	Plants	770
		Other	795
Costs	CS	Material	880
		Labour	890
		Overheads	900

Code the following costs, extracted from invoices and payroll, using the table below:

Cost	Code
• Purchase of seeds used to grow plants for resale.	
• External loans for investment in new greenhouses.	
• Wages of gardeners who maintain the plants to be sold.	
• Sales of food and drink.	

COST BEHAVIOUR

CALCULATION QUESTIONS

34   HULK PLC

Identify the type of cost behaviour (fixed, variable or semi-variable) described in each statement by putting a tick in the relevant column of the table below:

Statement	Fixed	Variable	Semi-variable
• Costs are £37,500 when 7,500 units are made and £62,500 when 12,500 units are made.			
• Costs are £2 per unit when 7,500 units are made and £1.20 per unit when 12,500 units are made.			
• Costs are £50,000 when 7,500 units are made and £80,000 when 12,500 units are made.			

35   BANNER PLC

Identify the type of cost behaviour (fixed, variable or semi-variable) described in each statement by putting a tick in the relevant column of the table below:

Statement	Fixed	Variable	Semi-variable
• Costs are £5,000 plus £45 per unit, regardless of the number of units made.			✓
• Costs are £5,000 when 300 units are made and £5,000 when 600 units are made.	✓		
• Costs are £35 per unit regardless of the number of units made.		✓	

36   NORTON PLC

Identify the type of cost behaviour (fixed, variable or semi-variable) described in each statement by putting a tick in the relevant column of the table below:

Statement	Fixed	Variable	Semi-variable
• Costs are £50,000 in total regardless of the number of units made.	✓		
• Costs are £50,000 in total when 2,500 units are made and £80,000 when 4,000 units are made.		✓	
• Costs are £7 per unit when 1,000 units are made and £6 per unit when 2,000 units are made.			✓

37   TRIUMPH LTD

Task 1

Identify the type of cost behaviour (fixed, variable or semi-variable) described in each statement by ticking the relevant boxes in the table below.

Statement	Fixed	Variable	Semi-variable
At 9,000 units this cost is £29,250, and at 12,000 units it is £39,000		✓	
At 5,000 units this cost is £5.20 per unit, and at 8,000 units it is £3.25 per unit			
At 19,800 units, this cost is £64,500, and at 27,000 units it is £82,500			✓

Task 2

Complete the table below by inserting all costs for activity levels of 6,000 and 14,000.

	6,000 units	7,000 units	10,000 units	14,000 units
Variable cost (£)				4,200 (11,400)
Fixed cost (£)	13,000			2,000
Total cost (£)		45,000	54,000	65,000

38   YOUNGS LTD

Task 1

Identify the type of cost behaviour (fixed, variable or semi-variable) described in each statement by ticking the relevant boxes in the table below.

Statement	Fixed	Variable	Semi-variable
At 4,000 units this cost is £3.00 per unit, and at 6,000 units it is £2.00 per unit.	✓		
At 7,000 units this cost is £32,500, and at 10,000 units it is £43,000.			✓
At 11,000 units this cost is £57,750, and at 15,000 units it is £78,750.		✓	

Task 2

Complete the table below by inserting all costs for activity levels of 8,000 and 16,000.

	8,000 units	10,000 units	13,000 units	16,000 units
Variable cost (£)	34000			68000
Fixed cost (£)	18000			18000
Total cost (£)	52000	60,500	73,250	86000

65500 ✗ (10000 × 2·25)

12430 = I·60500

39   CARE PLC

Task 1

Identify the type of cost behaviour (fixed, variable or semi-variable) described in each statement by ticking the relevant boxes in the table below.

Statement	Fixed	Variable	Semi-variable
At 8,000 units this cost is £38,000, and at 12,000 units it is £49,000			✓
At 10,500 units this cost is £39,375, and at 14,000 units it is £52,500		✓	
At 4,000 units this cost is £4.50 per unit, and at 6,000 units is £3.00 per unit	✓		

Task 2

Complete the table below by inserting all costs for activity levels of 3,000 and 12,000.

	3,000 units	5,000 units	9,000 units	12,000 units
Variable cost (£)				
Fixed cost (£)				
Total cost (£)		13,000	19,800	

40   ROBSHAW LTD

Task 1

Identify the type of cost behaviour (fixed, variable or semi-variable) described in each statement by ticking the relevant boxes in the table below.

Statement	Fixed	Variable	Semi-variable
At 6,000 units this cost is £3.75 per unit, and at 9,000 units it is £2.50 per unit	✓		
At 8,500 units this cost is £36,550, and at 11,300 units it is £48,590		✓	
At 11,000 units this cost is £27,750, and at 14,000 units it is £33,000			✓

Task 2

Complete the table below by inserting all costs for activity levels of 9,000 and 16,500.

	9,000 units	11,000 units	14,000 units	16,500 units
Variable cost (£)	29 250			53625
Fixed cost (£)	4500			4500
Total cost (£)	33 750	40,250	50,000	58125

NARRATIVE STYLE QUESTIONS

41   BUNGLE LTD

Bungle Ltd usually produces 9,000 units but is planning to increase production to 14,000 units during the next period.

Identify the following statements as either true or false by putting a tick in the relevant column of the table below:

Statement	True	False
• Total variable costs will decrease.		✓
• Total fixed costs will remain the same.	✓	
• The variable cost per unit will remain the same.	✓	
• The fixed cost per unit will increase.		✓

42   TF

Identify the following statements as either true or false by putting a tick in the relevant column of the table below:

Statement	True	False
• Variable costs change directly with changes in activity.	✓	
• Fixed costs change directly with changes in activity.		✓
• Stepped costs are fixed within a set range of output.	✓	

43   FIXED OR VARIABLE

Identify the following costs as either fixed or variable by putting a tick in the relevant column of the table below:

Cost	Fixed	Variable
• Direct materials.		✓
• Power used in production machinery.		✓
• Training costs for new employees in production.	✓	✗
• Insurance for sales cars.	✓	
• Insurance for machinery.	✓	
• Sales commission.	✗	✓

44 FOV

Identify the following costs as either fixed or variable by putting a tick in the relevant column of the table below:

Cost	Fixed	Variable
• Piecework wages paid to factory workers.		✓
• Salaries paid to company directors.	✓	
• Annual payment for cleaning of air conditioning units.	✓	

45 VOF

VOF is a company that prints magazines and newspapers.

Identify the following costs as either fixed or variable by putting a tick in the relevant column of the table below:

Cost	Fixed	Variable
• Annual salaries paid to factory managers.	✓	
• Hourly wages paid to factory workers.		✓
• Colour ink used to print magazines.		✓

46 STORM

Indicate whether each of the following costs is an overhead or not by putting a tick in the relevant column of the table below:

Cost	Overhead? Yes	Overhead? No
• Labour cost of workers who assemble the product.		✓
• Insurance cost of factory where product is assembled.	✓	
• Electricity for machinery.	✓	

47 ROGUE

Indicate whether each of the following costs is an overhead or not by putting a tick in the relevant column of the table below:

Cost	Overhead? Yes	Overhead? No
• Labour cost of cleaning staff in a factory.	✓	
• Depreciation of delivery vans.	✓	
• Cost of materials used to build the product.		✓

48   GAMBIT

Indicate whether each of the following costs is an overhead or not by putting a tick in the relevant column of the table below:

	Overhead?	
Cost	Yes	No
• Wages of staff paid on a piecework system.		✓
• Cost of factory canteen staff hourly wages.	✓	
• Direct materials.		✓

COST CARDS, TOTAL COSTS AND UNIT COSTS

49   JEEPERS LTD

Indicate whether the following costs are direct or not by putting a tick in the relevant column of the table below:

Cost	Yes	No
• Materials used in production.	✓	
• Piecework labour costs.	✓	
• Salary of chief executive.		✓

Jeepers Ltd makes a single product. At a production level of 15,000 units, the company has the following costs:

Materials   37,500 kilos at £14.00 per kilo   = 525000

Labour   7,500 hours at £16.00 per hour   = 126000

Overheads   £570,000   = 570000

Complete the table below to show the unit product cost at the production level of 15,000 units. Overheads are absorbed on a cost per unit basis. Give your answer to the nearest pound.

Element	Unit product cost
Materials	£ 35
Labour	£ 8
Direct cost	£ 43
Overheads	£ 38
Total	£ 81

50 BRANIAC LTD

Braniac Ltd makes a single product. A production level of 55,000 units has the following costs:

Materials	96,250 litres at £14 per litre
Labour	192,500 hours at £11.50 per hour
Overheads	£687,500

Complete the following unit cost table for a production level of 55,000 units. Overheads are absorbed on a cost per unit basis. Give your answer to the nearest penny.

Element	Unit cost
Materials	£ 24.50
Labour	£
Direct cost	£ 34.75
Overheads	£ 12.5
Total	£ 47.25

51 GLORIA LTD

Gloria Ltd is costing a single product which has the following cost details:

Variable costs per unit

Materials	£2
Labour	£3
Royalties	£0.50

Total fixed costs

Production overhead	£80,000
Sales and distribution	£90,000

Complete the following total cost and unit cost table for a production level of 20,000 units. Give your answer to the nearest penny for the unit cost and the nearest pound for the total cost.

Element	Unit cost	Total cost for 20,000 units
Variable production costs	£ 5.50 (2+3+0.50)	£ 110000
Fixed production costs	£ 4.00	£ 80,000
Total production cost	£ 9.50	£ 1,90,000

52 BIZARRO LTD

Bizarro Ltd makes a single product and for a production level of 17,000 units has the following cost details:

	Per unit	Cost
Materials	2.5kg	£18/kilo
Labour	1.0hrs	£9/hour
Fixed overheads		£42,500

Complete the table below to show the unit cost and total cost at the production level of 17,000 units. Overheads are absorbed on a cost per unit basis. Give your answer to the nearest penny for the unit cost and the nearest pound for total cost.

Element	Unit cost	Total cost
Materials	£ 45	£ 765000
Labour	£ 9	£ 153000
Overheads	£ 2.5	£ 42500
Total	£ 56.5	£ 960,500

53 VINNY LTD

Vinny Ltd is a commercial laundrette below are the costings for 15,000 units:

Variable costs

Materials	£75,000
Labour	£120,000

Fixed costs

Production overhead	£100,000

Complete the following total cost and unit cost table for a REVISED production level of 20,000 units. Give your answer to the nearest penny for the unit cost and the nearest pound for total cost.

Element	Unit cost	Total cost
Materials	£ 5	£ 100000
Labour	£ 8	£ 160,000
Overheads	£ 5	£ 100000
Total	£ 18	£ 360,000

54 DARKSEID LTD

Darkseid Ltd makes a single product and for a production level of 95,000 units has the following cost details:

Materials	47,500kg	at £7/kilo
Labour	71,250hrs	at £9/hour
Fixed overheads		£242,000

Complete the table below to show the unit cost at a REVISED production level of 100,000 units. Overheads are absorbed on a cost per unit basis. Give your answer to the nearest penny.

Element	Unit cost
Materials	£ 3.5
Labour	£ 6.75
Fixed overheads	£ 2.42
Total	£ 12.67

55 DOOMSDAY LTD

Doomsday Ltd is costing a single product which has the following cost details:

Variable costs per unit	Per unit	Cost
Materials	45kg	£0.50/kg
Labour	2.5hrs	£16/hour

Total fixed costs

Production overhead	£75,000
Administration overhead	£110,000
Sales and distribution	£75,000

Handwritten: M = 45 × '50 = 22·5 ; L = 40 = 40 + 22·5 = 62·5

Complete the following total cost and unit cost table for a production level of 20,000 units. Overheads are absorbed on a cost per unit basis. Give your answer to the nearest penny for the unit cost and the nearest pound for total cost.

Element	Total cost for 20,000 units	Unit cost
Direct costs	£ 1250000	£ 62·50
Production overhead	£ 75000	£ 3·75
Non production overhead	£ 110000 + 75000 = 185000	£ 9·25
Total costs	£ 1,510,000	£ 75·5

56 OLSEN LTD

Olsen Ltd is costing a single product which has the following cost details:

Variable costs	Per unit
Materials	£12
Labour	£17

Handwritten: Direct cost = M + L ; 19

Total Fixed Costs

Production overhead	£80,000
Administration overhead	£40,000

Complete the following total cost and unit cost table for a production level of 80,000 units. Give your answer to the nearest penny for the unit cost and the nearest pound for total cost.

Element	Total cost	Unit cost
Materials	£ 960,000	£ 12
Labour	£ 1360000	£ 17
Production overheads	£ 80,000	£ 1
Administration overheads	£ 40,000	£ 0·5
Total	£ 2440000	£ 30·5

57 FLAKEWAY LTD

Flakeway Ltd makes a single product and for a production level of 24,000 units has the following cost details:

Materials	6,000kg	at £20/kilo
Labour	8,000hrs	at £12/hour
Fixed overheads		£48,000

Complete the table below to show the unit cost at the production level of 24,000 units. Overheads are absorbed on a cost per unit basis. Give your answer to the nearest penny.

Element	Unit cost
Materials	£ 5
Labour	£ 4
Fixed overheads	£ 2
Total	£ 11

58 CORONATION LTD

Coronation Ltd is costing a single product which has the following cost details

Variable costs	Per unit	Cost
Materials	50g = 0.05 kg	£10/kg
Labour	1hr	£6/hour

Total fixed costs

Production overhead	£40,000
Administration overhead	£20,000
Sales and distribution	£25,000

Complete the following total cost and unit cost table for a production level of 5,000 units. Overheads are absorbed on a cost per unit basis. Give your answer to the nearest penny for the unit cost and the nearest pound for total cost.

Element	Total cost for 5,000 units	Unit cost
Direct costs	£ 200 X 6's = 32500	£ 6.05
Production overhead	£ 40000	£ 8
Non production overhead	£ 55000	£ 11
Total costs	£ 127500	£ 25.05

59 LUTHOR LTD

Luthor Ltd makes a single product and for a production level of 15,000 units has the following cost details:

Materials	60,000kg	at £15/kilo
Labour	37,500hrs	at £9/hour
Fixed overheads		£570,000

Complete the table below to show the unit cost at the production level of 15,000 units. Overheads are absorbed on a cost per unit basis. Give your answer to the nearest penny.

Element	Unit cost
Materials	£ 60
Labour	£ 22.5
Fixed overheads	£ 38
Total	£ 120.52

60 WILKINSON LTD

Wilkinson Ltd is looking to calculate the unit cost for one of the products it makes. It needs to calculate an overhead absorption rate to apply to each unit. The methods it is considering are a rate per machine hour, a rate per labour hour, and a rate per unit.

Total factory activity is forecast as follows:

Machine hours	10,000
Labour hours	12,500
Units	60,000
Overheads	£150,000

Task 1

Complete the table below to show the possible overhead absorption rates that Wilkinson Ltd could use. The absorption rates should be calculated to two decimal places.

	Machine hour	Labour hour	Unit
Overheads (£)	150,000	150,000	50000
Activity	10,000		
Absorption rate (£)	15	12	2.5

Task 2

The following data relates to making one unit of the product:

Material	2 kilos at £5 per kilo
Labour	15 minutes at £10 per hour
Production time	10 minutes

Complete the table below (to two decimal places) to calculate the total unit cost, using the three overhead absorption rates you have calculated in task 1.

Cost	Machine hour (£)	Labour hour (£)	Unit (£)
Material	10	10	10
Labour	2.5	2.5	2.5
Direct cost	12.5	12.5	12.5
Overheads	2.5	3	2.5
Total unit cost	15	15.5	15

61 HODGSON LTD

Hodgson Ltd is looking to calculate the unit cost for one of the products it makes. It needs to calculate an overhead absorption rate to apply to each unit. The methods it is considering are a rate per machine hour, a rate per labour hour, and a rate per unit.

Total factory activity is forecast as follows:

Machine hours	15,000
Labour hours	20,000
Units	100,000
Overheads	£250,000

Task 1

Complete the table below to show the possible overhead absorption rates that Hodgson Ltd could use. The absorption rates should be calculated to two decimal places.

	Machine hour	Labour hour	Unit
Overheads (£)	250,000	250,000	250,000
Activity	15,000	20,000	100,000
Absorption rate (£)	16·67	12·50	2·50

Task 2

The following data relates to making one unit of the product:

Material	4 kilos at £6 per kilo
Labour	30 minutes at £12 per hour
Production time	20 minutes

Complete the table below (to two decimal places) to calculate the total unit cost, using the three overhead absorption rates you have calculated in task 1.

Cost	Machine hour (£)	Labour hour (£)	Unit (£)
Material 4×6=24	24	24	24
Labour	6	6	6
Direct cost	⅓×16·67 30	30	30
Overheads	5·56	½ × 12·50 =6·25	2·50
Total unit cost	35·56	36·25	32·50

60m – 1h
1 m → 1/60

1/3 × 20 = 1/3 × 16·67

1 × 20 = 1/3
60

62   BARNES LTD

Barnes Ltd is looking to calculate the unit cost for one of the products it makes. It needs to calculate an overhead absorption rate to apply to each unit. The methods it is considering are a rate per machine hour, a rate per labour hour, and a rate per unit.

Total factory activity is forecast as follows:

Machine hours	17,500
Labour hours	12,000
Units	40,000
Overheads	£130,000

Task 1

Complete the table below to show the possible overhead absorption rates that Barnes Ltd could use. The absorption rates should be calculated to two decimal places.

	Machine hour	Labour hour	Unit
Overheads (£)	130000	130000	130000
Activity	17500	12000	4000
Absorption rate (£)	7.43	10.83	3.25

Task 2

The following data relates to making one unit of the product:

Material	3 kilos at £5 per kilo
Labour	20 minutes at £15 per hour $\frac{20}{60} \times 15$
Production time	30 minutes

Complete the table below (to two decimal places) to calculate the total unit cost, using the three overhead absorption rates you have calculated in task 1.

Cost	Machine hour (£)	Labour hour (£)	Unit (£)
Material 5×3	15	15	15
Labour	5	5	5
Direct cost	$\frac{30}{60}$ 20 =	20	20
Overheads	$\frac{30}{60} \times 7.43 = 3.72$	$\frac{20}{60} \times 10.83 = 3.61$	3.25
Total unit cost	23.72	20.61	23.25

63 ANDREW LTD

Andrew Ltd is looking to calculate the unit cost for one of the products it makes. It needs to calculate an overhead absorption rate to apply to each unit. The methods it is considering are a rate per machine hour, a rate per labour hour, and a rate per unit.

Total factory activity is forecast as follows:

Machine hours	9,000
Labour hours	11,000
Units	60,000
Overheads	£145,000

Task 1

Complete the table below to show the possible overhead absorption rates that Andrew Ltd could use. The absorption rates should be calculated to two decimal places.

	Machine hour	Labour hour	Unit
Overheads (£)			
Activity			
Absorption rate (£)			

Task 2

The following data relates to making one unit of the product:

Material	1 kilo at £8 per kilo
Labour	30 minutes at £14 per hour
Production time	20 minutes

Complete the table below (to two decimal places) to calculate the total unit cost, using the three overhead absorption rates you have calculated in task 1.

Cost	Machine hour (£)	Labour hour (£)	Unit (£)
Material			
Labour			
Direct cost			
Overheads			
Total unit cost			

MANUFACTURING ACCOUNTS

64 JOKER LTD

Reorder the following costs into a manufacturing account format on the right side of the table below for the year ended 31 December.

	£		£
Closing inventory of work in progress	52,000	OI RM	50,000
Direct labour	140,000	PofR M	120000
Opening inventory of raw materials	50,000	ClofRM	(65,000)
Closing inventory of finished goods	61,000	DMU	105000
Closing inventory of raw materials	65,000	DL	140,000
Manufacturing overheads	85,000	DC	245000
COST OF GOODS SOLD		MOV	85000
MANUFACTURING COST		MC	330000
Purchases of raw materials	120,000	OIWIP	48000
Opening inventory of work in progress	48,000	CIWIP	(52000)
Opening inventory of finished goods	57,000	Cof GoodsM	326000
DIRECT COST		OIFG	57000
DIRECT MATERIALS USED		CIFG	(61,000)
COST OF GOODS MANUFACTURED		Costofgoods	322000

Enter the correct figures for the following costs which were not provided in the table above.

	£
DIRECT MATERIALS USED	105000
DIRECT COST	245000
MANUFACTURING COST	330000
COST OF GOODS MANUFACTURED	326000
COST OF GOODS SOLD	322000

OI RM
PI RM
CI RM
DMU
DL
DC
MO
MC
OIWIP
CIWIP
COGM
OIFG
CIFG
costof g.

OC
P
C
DMU
DL
DC
MO
MC
O
C
C
O

65   TUT LTD

Reorder the following costs into a manufacturing account format on the right side of the table below for the year ended 31 July.

	£		£
COST OF GOODS MANUFACTURED		OIRM	10000
Opening inventory of work in progress	12,000	PIRM	60,000
Opening inventory of raw materials	10,000	CIRM	(12000)
COST OF GOODS SOLD		DMU	58000
Closing inventory of finished goods	20,000	DL	88000
Closing inventory of raw materials	12,000	DC	146000
Manufacturing overheads	45,000	MO	45000
MANUFACTURING COST		ML	191000
Purchases of raw materials	60,000	OIWIP	12000
Opening inventory of finished goods	18,000	CIWIR	(15000)
DIRECT COST		CoGMN	188000
Direct labour	88,000	OIFG	18000
Closing inventory of work in progress	15,000	CIFG	(20000)
DIRECT MATERIALS USED		C oGoS	

Enter the correct figures for the following costs which were not provided in the table above.

	£
DIRECT MATERIALS USED	58000
DIRECT COST	146000
MANUFACTURING COST	191000
COST OF GOODS MANUFACTURED	188000
COST OF GOODS SOLD	186000

66 RIDDLER LTD

Reorder the following costs into a manufacturing account format on the right side of the table below for the year ended 31 May. Enter the correct figures for the costs in bold that are not provided.

	£		£
DIRECT COST		*oI RM*	*14000*
Closing inventory of raw materials	20,000	*PRM*	*100,000*
Closing inventory of work in progress	20,000	*c I RM*	*(20000)*
Opening inventory of finished goods	60,000	*DMU*	*94000*
Direct labour	194,000	*DL*	*194000*
Closing inventory of finished goods	50,000	*DC*	*288000*
Manufacturing overheads	106,000	*MO*	*106000*
Purchases of raw materials	100,000	*MCost*	*394000*
Opening inventory of work in progress	16,000	*OIWIP*	*16000*
COST OF GOODS SOLD		*c IWP*	*(20,000)*
DIRECT MATERIALS USED		*C oGM*	*390000*
Opening inventory of raw materials	14,000	*OIFG*	*60,000*
MANUFACTURING COST		*c IFG*	*(50,000)*
COST OF GOODS MANUFACTURED		*Cost of Goods Sold*	*400,000*

67 CLOCKING LTD

Reorder the following costs into a manufacturing account format on the right side of the table below for the year ended 31 May. Enter the correct figures for the costs in bold that are not provided.

	£		£
Closing inventory of work in progress	10,000		
Direct labour	97,000		
Opening inventory of raw materials	7,000		
Closing inventory of finished goods	25,000		
Closing inventory of raw materials	10,000		
Manufacturing overheads	53,000		
COST OF GOODS SOLD			
MANUFACTURING COST			
Purchases of raw materials	50,000		
Opening inventory of work in progress	8,000		
Opening inventory of finished goods	30,000		
DIRECT COST			
DIRECT MATERIALS USED			
COST OF GOODS MANUFACTURED			

68   BOOKWORM LTD

Reorder the following costs into a manufacturing account format on the right side of the table below for the year ended 31 December. Enter the correct figures for the costs in bold that are not provided.

	£		£
DIRECT COST			
Direct labour	15,000		
MANUFACTURING COST			
Opening inventory of raw materials	5,000		
Closing inventory of finished goods	16,000		
Purchases of raw materials	15,000		
DIRECT MATERIALS USED			
Manufacturing overheads	25,000		
Closing inventory of raw materials	8,000		
COST OF GOODS SOLD			
COST OF GOODS MANUFACTURED			
Opening inventory of finished goods	12,000		
Opening inventory of work in progress	4,000		
Closing inventory of work in progress	6,000		

69   MULTI

Within a manufacturing account, the manufacturing costs are £45,000. Opening work in progress is £11,000, while opening finished goods were costed at £8,100. Closing work in progress is £9,700, while closing finished goods were £8,900.

What is Multi's cost of goods sold?

A   £44,500

B   £48,700

C   £45,500

D   £41,300

COSTING FOR INVENTORY AND WORK-IN-PROGRESS

NARRATIVE STYLE QUESTIONS

70 BOBBLE LTD

Match the disadvantage to the method of stock valuation by placing a tick in the relevant column of the table below:

Characteristic	FIFO	LIFO	AVCO
• Potentially out of date valuation on issues.	✓		
• The valuation of inventory rarely reflects the actual purchase price of the material.			✓
• Potentially out of date closing inventory valuation.		✓	

71 LINT LTD

Identify the following statements as either true or false by putting a tick in the relevant column of the table below:

Statement	True	False
• In periods of rising prices, FIFO gives a higher valuation of closing inventory than LIFO or AVCO.	✓	
• In periods of falling prices, LIFO gives a higher valuation of issues of inventory than FIFO or AVCO.		✓
• AVCO would normally be expected to produce a valuation of closing inventory somewhere between valuations under FIFO and LIFO.	✓	

72 FLUFF LTD

Identify the correct inventory valuation method from the characteristic given by putting a tick in the relevant column of the table below:

Characteristic	FIFO	LIFO	AVCO
• This inventory valuation method is particularly suited to inventory that consist of liquid materials e.g. oil.			✓
• This inventory valuation method is particularly suited to inventory that has a short shelf life e.g. dairy products.	✓		
• This inventory valuation method is suited to a wheat farmer who has large silos of grain. Grain is added to and taken from the top of these silos.		✓	

73 FIDO LTD

Identify the correct inventory valuation method from the characteristic given by putting a tick in the relevant column of the table below:

Characteristic	FIFO	LIFO	AVCO
• In times of rising prices this method will give higher profits.	✓		
• In times of rising prices this method will give lower profits.		✓	
• In times of rising prices this method gives a middle level of profits compared to the other two.			✓

74 TRUFFEAUX LTD

Identify whether the following statements are true or false by putting a tick in the relevant column of the table below:

Statement	True	False
• FIFO costs issues of inventory at the most recent purchase price.		✓
• AVCO costs issues of inventory at the oldest purchase price.		✓
• LIFO costs issues of inventory at the oldest purchase price.		✓
• FIFO values closing inventory at the most recent purchase price.	✓	
• LIFO values closing inventory at the most recent purchase price.		✓
• AVCO values closing inventory at the latest purchase price.		✓

75 STOCKY LTD

Identify the correct inventory valuation method from the characteristic given by putting a tick in the relevant column of the table below:

Characteristic	FIFO	LIFO	AVCO
• Issues are valued at the most recent purchase cost.		✓	
• Inventory is valued at the average of the cost of purchases.			✓
• Inventory is valued at the most recent purchase cost.	✓		

IDENTIFICATION OF INVENTORY VALUATION METHOD

76 EPIC LTD

You are told that the opening inventory of a single raw material in the stores is 8,000 units at £5 per unit. During the month, 12,000 units at £4.50 were received and the following week 14,000 units were issued.

Task 1

Identify the valuation method described in the statements below:

Characteristic	FIFO	LIFO	AVCO
• Closing inventory is valued at £28,200.			✓
• The issue of inventory is valued at £67,000.	✓		
• The issue of inventory is valued at £64,000.		✓	

Task 2

Identify whether the statements in the table below are true or false by putting a tick in the relevant column.

	True	False
• AVCO values the issue of inventory at £65,800.	✓	
• LIFO values the closing inventory at £27,000.		✓
• FIFO values the closing inventory at £30,000.		✓

77 AWESOME LTD

You are told that the opening inventory of a single raw material in the stores is 6,000 units at £6 per unit. During the month, another 6,000 units at £10 were received and the following week 7,150 units were issued.

Task 1

Identify the valuation method described in the statements below:

Characteristic	FIFO	LIFO	AVCO
• Closing inventory is valued at £48,500.	✓		
• The issue of inventory is valued at £57,200.			✓
• The issue of inventory is valued at £66,900.		✓	

Task 2

Identify whether the statements in the table below are true or false by putting a tick in the relevant column.

	True	False
• FIFO values the issue of inventory at £47,500.	✓	
• AVCO values the closing inventory at £38,400.		✓
• LIFO values the closing inventory at £29,100.	✓	

78 AMAZING LTD

You are told that the opening inventory of a single raw material in the stores is 2,000 units at £1.50 per unit. During the month, another 5,000 units at £5 were received and the following week 6,000 units were issued.

Task 1

Identify the valuation method described in the statements below:

Characteristic	FIFO	LIFO	AVCO
• Closing inventory is valued at £1,500.		✓	
• The issue of inventory is valued at £23,000.	✓		
• The issue of inventory is valued at £24,000.			✓

Task 2

Identify whether the statements in the table below are true or false by putting a tick in the relevant column.

	True	False
• LIFO values the issue of inventory at £26,500.	✓	
• AVCO values the closing inventory at £5,000.		✓
• LIFO values the closing inventory at £4,000.		✓

INVENTORY CARDS

79 STONE LTD

Stone Ltd sells stone to builders. It had the following movements in one type of stone for the month of June.

DATE	RECEIPTS		ISSUES	
	Tonnes	Cost	Tonnes	Cost
June 1	500	£7,500		
June 8	350	£6,125		
June 15	275	£4,950		
June 22			650	
June 29	500	£8,750		

Complete the table below for the issue and closing inventory values, stating your answers to the nearest pound.

Method	Cost of issue on 22 June	Closing inventory at 30 June
FIFO	£	£
LIFO	£	£
AVCO	£	£

80   NATAL LTD

IMP

Natal Ltd makes and sells a wide range of clothes for babies. The following is an inventory card for Natal's most popular product for the month of December.

DATE	RECEIPTS		ISSUES	
	Units	Cost	Units	Cost
December 3	10,000	£85,000		
December 18	14,000	£112,000		
December 19	50,000	£350,000		
December 25			72,500	
December 29	5,000	£30,000		

Task 1

Complete the table below for the issue and closing inventory values. Give your answers to the nearest pound.

Method	Cost of issue on 25 Dec	Closing inventory at 29 Dec
LIFO	£	£
AVCO	£	£

Task 2

Identify the following statements as true or false by putting a tick in the relevant column of the table below:

	True	False
• FIFO would give a lower closing inventory valuation on the 29 December than LIFO and AVCO.	✓	
• FIFO would give a lower cost of issue on the 25 December than LIFO and AVCO.		✓

81   GANDALF LTD

Gandalf Ltd has the following movements in a certain type of inventory into and out of its stores for the month of July.

DATE	RECEIPTS			ISSUES			BALANCE
	Units	Unit cost	Total £	Units	Unit cost	Total £	Total £
July 2	600	£1.50	£900				
July 4	500	£1.70	£850				
July 15				620			
July 19	200	£1.80	£360				
July 31				400			

Calculate the costs of the issues made on July 15 and July 31 if Gandalf plc uses a LIFO inventory valuation method.

	Valuation £
• July 15	
• July 31	

82 GRUNDY LTD

Grundy Ltd has the following movements in a certain type of inventory into and out of its stores for the month of October.

DATE	RECEIPTS		ISSUES	
	Units	Cost	Units	Cost
October 9	6000	£15,000	2·5	
October 12	3000	£6,000	2	
October 20	3000	£3,000	1	
October 25			8500	
October 30	1000	£1,500		

25500

Complete the table below for the issue and closing inventory values.

Method	Cost of issue on 25 October	Closing inventory at 31 October
FIFO 15000 + 2500X2	£ 20,000	£ 5500
LIFO 3000 + 6000 + 2500×2½	£ 9000 + 6250 = 15250	£ 10250
AVCO 24000/12000 = 2	£ 2×8500 = 17000	£ 8500

83 LOBO LTD

Lobo Ltd has the following movements in a certain type of inventory into and out of its stores for the month of May.

DATE	RECEIPTS		ISSUES	
	Units	Cost	Units	Cost
May 12	250	£1,375	5·5	
May 17	400	£1,800	4·5	
May 18	600	£1,200	2·0	
May 29			500	
May 30	100	£375	3·75	

4750

(250×5·5)+(250×4·5) = 1375+1125 FIFO

500 × 2 =

Complete the table below for the issue and closing inventory values.

Method	Cost of issue on 29 May	Closing inventory at 30 May
FIFO	£ *2500*	£ *2250*
LIFO	£ *500 x 2 = 1,0970*	£ *1000 → 4750 = 3750*
AVCO	£ *4375/1250 = 3'5 x 500 / 1750*	£ *3000*

84 ZOD LTD

1375 + 250 x 45 = 2500+

Zod Ltd has the following movements in a certain type of inventory into and out of it stores for the month of February.

DATE	RECEIPTS		ISSUES	
	Units	Cost	Units	Cost
February 2	100	£500	*5*	
February 3	*50*	*250*	50	
February 12	150	£600	*4*	
February 16			60	
February 20	110	£505		
February 26			40	

1605

Complete the table below for the issue and closing inventory values. State your answer to the nearest pound.

Method	Cost of issue on 16 February	Closing inventory at 26 February
FIFO	£	£ *408*
AVCO	£	£

COSTING FOR LABOUR

210

NARRATIVE STYLE QUESTIONS

85 NULAB LTD

Identify the labour payment method by putting a tick in the relevant column of the table below:

Payment method	Time-rate	Piecework	Piece-rate plus bonus
• Labour is paid based solely on the production achieved.		✓	
• Labour is paid extra if an agreed level of output is exceeded.			✓
• Labour is paid according to hours worked.	✓		

86   LU LTD

Identify one advantage for each labour payment method by putting a tick in the relevant column of the table below:

Payment method	Time-rate	Piecework	Time-rate plus bonus
• Assured level of remuneration for employee.	✓		
• Employee earns more if they work more efficiently than expected.		✓	
• Assured level of remuneration and reward for working efficiently.			✓

87   MANDELA LTD

Identify whether the following statements are true or false in the relevant column of the table below:

Statement	True	False
• Time rate is paid based on the production achieved.		✓
• Overtime is paid for hours worked over the standard hours agreed.	✓	
• Piece rate is paid according to hours worked.		✓

88   PERRES LTD

Identify the hourly payment method by putting a tick in the relevant column of the table below:

Payment method	Basic rate	Overtime premium	Overtime rate
• This is the amount paid above the basic rate for hours worked in excess of the normal hours.		✓	
• This is the total amount paid per hour for hours worked in excess of the normal hours.			✓
• This is the amount paid per hour for normal hours worked.	✓		

89 TEVEZ LTD

Identify the following statements as true or false by putting a tick in the relevant column of the table below:

Statement	True	False
• Direct labour costs can be identified with the goods being made or the service being provided.	✓	
• Indirect labour costs vary directly with the level of activity.		✓

90 BERDYCH LTD

Identify the whether the labour payment is usually associated with a fixed or variable cost by putting a tick in the relevant column of the table below:

Payment method	Variable	Fixed
• Labour that is paid based on a time rate basis per hour worked.	✓	
• Labour is paid on a monthly salary basis.		✓
• Labour that is based on number of units produced.	✓	

91 SODERLING LTD

Identify each labour payment method by putting a tick in the relevant column of the table below:

Payment method	Time-rate	Piecework	Salary
• Assured level of remuneration for employee usually agreed for the year.			✓
• Employee earnings are directly linked with units they produce.		✓	
• Employee earnings are directly linked with hours they work.	✓		

92 MURRAY LTD

Identify the following statements as true or false by putting a tick in the relevant column of the table below:

	True	False
• Indirect labour costs includes production supervisors' salaries.	✓	
• Direct labour costs usually vary directly with the level of activity.	✓	

93 OWEN LTD

Identify one advantage for each labour payment method by putting a tick in the relevant column of the table below:

Payment method	Time-rate	Piecework	Salary
• Employee is paid the same amount every month.			✓
• Employee wage increases in direct correlation with the number of hours worked.	✓		
• Employee wage increases in direct correlation with the number of units produced.		✓	

94 PIECEWORK STATEMENTS

Identify the following statements as either true or false by putting a tick in the relevant column of the table below:

Statement	True	False
• Piecework encourages employees to work harder.	✓	
• Piecework requires accurate recording of the number of hours staff have worked.		✓
• Piecework encourages workers to improve the quality of the units they produce.		✓

CALCULATING LABOUR COSTS

95 MUTANT LTD

Mutant Ltd pays a time-rate of £7.50 per hour to its direct labour for a standard 32 hour week. Any of the labour force working in excess of 32 hours is paid an overtime rate of time and a half.

Calculate the following figures for the week for the two workers in the table below, entering your answers to the nearest pound.

Worker	Hours worked	Basic wage	Overtime	Gross wage
S. Torm	34 hours	£ 240	£ 11·25×2	£ 262·50
J. Grey	38 hours	£ 240	£ 11·25×2	£ 285

96   PHOENIX LTD

Phoenix plc pays its employees £8.00 per hour and expects them to make 20 units per hour. Any excess production will be paid a bonus of £1.50 per unit.

Identify the following statements as being true or false by putting a tick in the relevant column of the table below:

Statement	True	False
An employee who works 38 hours and makes 775 units will not receive a bonus.		✓
An employee who works 40 hours and makes 815 units will receive total pay of £342.50.	✓	
An employee who works 37 hours and makes 744 units will earn a bonus of £6.	✓	✓

97   KAHN LTD

Kahn Ltd uses a time-rate method with bonus to pay its direct labour in one of its factories. The time-rate used is £12 per hour and a worker is expected to produce 5 units an hour, any time saved is paid at £6 per hour.

Calculate the gross wage for the week including bonus for the three workers in the table below:

Worker	Hours worked	Units produced	Basic wage	Bonus	Gross wage
A. Smith	35	175	£ 420	£ 0	£ 420
J. O'Hara	35	180	£ 420	£ 6	£ 426
M.Stizgt	35	185	£ 420	£ 12	£ 432

98   ENTERPRISE LTD

Enterprise Ltd pays a time-rate of £12 per hour to its direct labour force for a standard 35 hour week. Any of the labour force working in excess of 35 hours is paid an overtime rate of time and a half.

Calculate the gross wage for the week for the three workers in the table below:

Worker	Hours worked	Basic wage	Overtime	Gross wage
J. Picard	37 hours	£ 420	£ 2×18	£ 456
B. Crusher	42 hours	£ 420	£ 7×18	£ 546
D. Troi	31 hours	£ 372	£ 0	£ 372

99 SGC LTD

Imp

SGC Ltd uses a basic salary plus piecework method to pay labour in one of its factories. The basic salary is £285 per week the piece rate used is £0.75 per unit produced.

Calculate the gross wage for the week for the two workers in the table below. Enter your answer to the nearest penny.

Worker	Units produced in week	Gross wage
J. O'Neill	500 units	£ 375 + 285 = 660
S. Carter	650 units	£ 437.5 + 285

772.5

100 GOTHIC LTD

Gothic Ltd uses a time-rate method with bonus to pay its direct labour in one of its factories. The time-rate used is £17 per hour and a worker is expected to produce 8 units an hour, anything over this and the worker is paid a bonus of £5 per unit.

Calculate the gross wage for the week including bonus for the three workers in the table below:

Worker	Hours worked	Units produced	Basic wage	Bonus	Gross wage
M. Shelley	37	300 = 296	£ 629	£ 20	£ 649
G. Leroux	37	312 = 16	£ 629	£ 80	£ 709
E. A. Poe	37	296	£ 629	£ 0	£ 629

101 AVENGERS LTD

Avengers Ltd pays a time-rate of £10 per hour to its direct labour force a standard 35 hour week. Any of the labour force working in excess of this over the four week period is paid an overtime rate of time and a quarter.

Calculate the gross wage for the **4-week** period for the three workers in the table below. Enter your answers to the nearest pound.

Worker	Hours worked	Basic wage	Overtime	Gross wage
T. Stark 35×4 = 140	138 ×10	£ 1380	£ 0	£ 1380
B. Banner = 140	142 ×10	£ 1400	£ 2 × 12.5 = 25	£ 1425
S. Rogers = 140	145 =	£ 1400	£ 5 × 12.5 = 62.5	£ 1463

102 DRACO LTD

Draco Ltd uses a piecework method to pay labour in one of its factories. The rate used is 80p per unit produced up to the standard number of units to be produced per week of 250. For any units over that the workers will get £10 per 20 units.

Calculate the gross wage for the week for the three workers in the table below:

Worker	Units produced in week	Gross wage
P. Jones	240 units	£
D. Bannatyne	350 units	£
L. Redford	250 units	£

103 QUAGGA PLC

Quagga plc pays its employees £4.50 per hour and expects them to make 50 units per hour. Any excess production will be paid a bonus of 45p per unit.

Identify the following statements as being true or false by putting a tick in the relevant column of the table below:

Statement	True	False
During a 29 hour week, an employee producing 1,475 units would not receive a bonus.		
During a 32 hour week, an employee producing 1,665 units would receive a bonus of £29.25.		
During a 37 hour week, an employee producing 1,925 units would receive total pay of £300.25.		

104 JLA PLC

JLA plc pays its employees £5 per hour and expects them to make 6 units per hour. Any time saved will be paid as a bonus at £8 per hour.

Identify the following statements as being true or false by putting a tick in the relevant column of the table below:

Statement	True	False
During a 30 hour week, an employee producing 192 units would receive a bonus of £16.		
During a 35 hour week, an employee producing 240 units would receive total pay of £215.		
During a 30 hour week, an employee producing 180 units would not receive a bonus.		

105 INJUSTICE LTD

Davidson Ltd pays a basic wage of £175/week plus £1.20 per unit produced.

Calculate the gross wage for the week for the three workers in the table below:

Worker	Units produced	Basic wage	Piece work	Gross wage
N. Wing	295	£ 175	£ 354	£ 529
W. Woman	355	£ 175	£ 426	£ 601
T. Flash	385	£ 175	£ 462	£ 637

106 GREENWOOD LTD

Greenwood Ltd pays a basic wage of £350/week equivalent to a time-rate of £10 per hour and a standard 35 hour week. Workers are expected to produce 5 units an hour and for units produced in excess of this a bonus is paid based on £7 for every hour saved.

So, for example, if 10 additional units are produced, then this would be equivalent to two hours saved and a bonus of £14 awarded.

5 + 5 = 10 unit
7 + 7 = £14 awarded

Calculate the gross wage for the week including bonus for the three workers in the table below:

Worker	Hours worked	Units produced	Basic wage	Bonus	Gross wage
B. Ryan	35	175	£ 350	£ 0	£ 350
S. Chang	35 190-175=15 190-175	£ 350	£ 21	£ 371
E. Schneider	35 210-175=35 210-175	£ 350	£ 49	£ 399

15 ÷ 5 = 3
= 3 × 7 = 21
35 ÷ 5 = 7 = 7 × 7 = 49

VARIANCES

NARRATIVE QUESTIONS

107 VARIOUS LTD

Identify the following statements as being true or false by putting a tick in the relevant column of the table below:

Statement	True	False
• A variance is the difference between budgeted and actual cost.	✓	
• A favourable variance could arise due to actual costs being less than budgeted.	✓	
• An adverse variance could arise due to actual income being less than budgeted.	✓	
• A favourable variance occurs when actual income is the same as budgeted income.		✓

108 JONES LTD

Identify the following statements as being true or false by putting a tick in the relevant column of the table below:

Statement	True	False
If budgeted sales are 6,000 units at £7.50 per unit and actual sales are £47,600, the sales variance is favourable	✓	
A favourable cost variance occurs when an actual cost of £9,800 is compared to a budgeted cost of £24 per unit for a budgeted output of 400 units	'	✓
A variance arises from a comparison of budgeted costs for last year with actual costs for this year	'	✓
If actual material costs are the same as budgeted costs for materials then no variance arises	✓	

109 GATLAND LTD

Identify the following statements as being true or false by putting a tick in the relevant column of the table below:

Statement	True	False
If budgeted sales are 4,000 units at £9.50 per unit and actual sales are £35,200, the sales variance is favourable		✓
A favourable cost variance occurs when an actual cost of £6,400 is compared to a budgeted cost of £14 per unit for a budgeted output of 500 units 7000	✓	'
A variance arises from a comparison of budgeted costs for last year with budgeted costs for this year	'	✓
If actual material costs are the same as budgeted costs for materials then the materials variance is adverse		✓

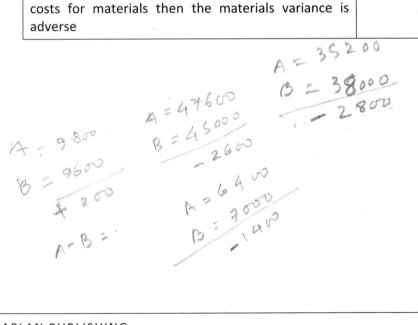

110 LANCASTER LTD

Identify the following statements as being true or false by putting a tick in the relevant column of the table below:

Statement	True	False
If budgeted sales are 14,000 units at £3.50 per unit and actual sales are £45,200, the sales variance is favourable		✓
An adverse cost variance occurs when an actual cost of £68,400 is compared to a budgeted cost of £14 per unit for a budgeted output of 5,000 units		✓
A variance arises from a comparison of budgeted costs for this year with actual costs for this year	✓	
If actual material costs are the same as budgeted costs for materials then the materials variance is favourable		✓

111 GOODE LTD

Identify the following statements as being true or false by putting a tick in the relevant column of the table below:

Statement	True	False
The variance for the Direct Material cost of Department B should be reported to the purchasing manager		
The variance for the Direct Labour cost for Department A should be reported to the sales manager		
The variance for the Direct Labour cost for Department B should be reported to the production manager of Department A		
A Direct Material cost variance that has been deemed Not Significant should not be reported		

112 BROWN LTD

Identify the following statements as being true or false by putting a tick in the relevant column of the table below:

Statement	True	False
The variance for the Direct Material cost of Department A should be reported to the purchasing manager		
The variance for the Direct Labour cost for Department A should be reported to the production manager of Department B		
The variance for sales should be reported to the sales manager		
A Direct Material cost variance that has been deemed Significant should not be reported		

VARIANCE CALCULATION QUESTIONS

113 EREBOR PLC

Erebor Ltd has produced a performance report detailing budgeted and actual cost for last month.

Calculate the amount of the variance for each cost type and then determine whether it is adverse or favourable (enter A or F).

Cost type	Budget £	Actual £	Variance £	Adverse or favourable (A or F)
Sales	600,500	597,800	2700	A
Direct materials	205,800	208,500	–2700	A
Direct labour	155,000	154,800	200	F
Production overheads	65,000	72,100	7100	A
Administration overheads	58,400	55,200	–3200	F

114 MORIA LTD

The following performance report for this month has been produced for Moria Ltd. Any variance in excess of 7% of budget is deemed to be significant.

Calculate the variance as a % of the budget and enter your answer into the table below to the **nearest whole percentage**. Indicate whether the variance is significant or not by entering S for significant and NS for not significant.

Cost type	Budget	Variance	Variance as % of budget	Significant or Not significant
Sales	45,100	4,214	$\frac{0.09 \times 100}{=9}$	S
Material	15,750	1,260	$\frac{0.08 \times 100}{=8}$	S
Labour	12,915	805	$\frac{0.06 \times 100}{=6}$	NS
Variable overheads	5,750	315	$\frac{0.05 \times 100}{=5}$	NS
Fixed overheads	8,155	1,011	$\frac{0.12 \times 100}{=12}$	S

Handwritten margin notes:
S 7 < 9·34
NS 7 < 8
NS 7 > 6·23
NS 7 > 6·48
7 < 12·39

·09 > 7%
8 > 7
6 < 7
5 < 7
12 > 7

115 WYEDALE LTD

Wyedale Ltd has produced a performance report detailing budgeted and actual cost for last month.

Calculate the amount of the variance in £ and % for each cost type and then determine whether it is adverse or favourable by putting an A or F in the relevant column of the table below. State your percentage to the nearest whole number.

Cost type	Budget £	Actual £	Variance £	Variance %	Adverse/ Favourable
Sales	27,000	29,775	2775	$\frac{0.10 \times 100}{10}$	F
Direct materials	7,400	8,510	1110	$\frac{0.15 \times 100}{=15}$	A
Direct labour	7,200	7,920	720	$\frac{0.1 \times 100}{10}$	A
Production overheads	5,500	5,390	110	$\frac{0.02 \times 100}{=2}$	F
Administration overheads	4,500	4,365	135	$\frac{0.03 \times 100}{=3}$	F

116 BELEGOST LTD

Problem with Adverse or favourable

The following performance report for this month has been produced for Belegost Ltd as summarised in the table below. Any variance in excess of 6% of budget is deemed to be significant and should be reported to the relevant manager for review and appropriate action.

Determine whether the variance for each figure is adverse or favourable by putting an A or F into the relevant column of the table below. Put an S in the relevant column if the variance is significant or an NS if the variance is not significant.

	Budget £	Actual £	Adverse or Favourable (A or F)	Significant or not significant (S or NS)
Sales	205,000	207,100	2100	NS
Direct materials	75,150	78,750	3600	NS
Direct labour	110,556	107,950	2606	NS
Production overheads	14,190	12,500	1690	S
Non-production overheads	16,190	17,880	1690	S

1 < 6
4 < 6
2 < 6
11 > 6
10 > 6

117 IVAN LTD

Ivan Ltd has produced a performance report detailing budgeted and actual cost for last month.

Calculate the amount of the variance for each cost type and then determine whether it is adverse or favourable by putting an A or an F into the relevant column below:

Cost type	Budget £	Actual £	Variance £	Adverse or Favourable (A or F)
Sales	544,750	547,450	2700	F
Direct materials	76,800	80,200	3400	A
Direct labour	148,400	146,000	2400	F
Production overheads	136,000	144,200	8200	A
Administration overheads	105,000	109,800	4800	A

118   BLUEBELL LTD

The following performance report for this month has been produced for Bluebell Ltd as summarised in the table below.

Calculate the variances in the table below and indicate whether they are adverse or favourable by putting an A or F in the relevant column and calculate the variance as a % to the nearest whole number.

Cost type	Budget £	Actual £	Variance £	Adverse/ Favourable	%
Sales	£204,555	£197,455	7100	A	43
Direct materials	£39,000	£42,300	3300	A	88
Direct labour	£75,000	£83,000	8000	A	11
Production overheads	£69,000	£64,800	4200	F	6·008
Administration overheads	£53,000	£58,900	5900	A	11·13

Section 2

ANSWERS TO PRACTICE QUESTIONS

COST CLASSIFICATION

FINANCIAL AND MANAGEMENT ACCOUNTING

1   FAMA

Characteristic	Financial accounting	Management accounting
• Have to be produced annually.	✓	
• Analyses historic events to help produce forecasts.		✓
• Is always produced using accounting standards.	✓	
• Is produced on an ad hoc basis when required.		✓

2   FINANCIAL AND MANAGEMENT

Characteristic	Financial accounting	Management accounting
• Must be presented as specified by the Companies Act and accounting standards.	✓	
• Helps managers run the business on a day-to-day basis.		✓
• Used as the basis for the calculation of the organisation's tax charge.	✓	
• Can include anything that managers feel is useful for the business.		✓

3 MAFA

Characteristic	Management accounting	Financial accounting
• It is based on past events.		✓
• Its purpose is to provide information for managers.	✓	
• It is based on future events.	✓	
• It complies with company law and accounting rules.		✓

4 FEATURES

Feature	Financial accounting	Management accounting
• Analysis of profit by cost centre.		✓
• Statement of profit or loss using format as dictated by accounting standards and company law.	✓	
• Cash flow forecasts.		✓
• Cost per unit calculation.		✓

COST AND PROFIT CENTRES

5 JEREMY

	Cost centre	Profit centre
• Bakery	✓	
• Shop		✓
• Office	✓	

6 PRINT PLC

Department	Cost centre	Profit centre
• Binding		✓
• Shops		✓
• Marketing	✓	

7 HOOCH PLC

Department	Cost centre	Profit centre	Investment centre
• Hooch's manager has no responsibility for income or asset purchases and disposals.	✓		
• Hooch's manager is assessed on the profitability of their department, as well as how effectively they have controlled their assets.			✓
• Hooch's manager is responsible for income and expenditure of their department only.		✓	

CLASSIFYING COSTS BY ELEMENT (MATERIALS, LABOUR OR OVERHEADS)

8 VVV LTD

Cost	Materials	Labour	Overheads
• Paint used on the planes.	✓		
• Depreciation of the machines used in the factory.			✓
• Oil used on the machines in the factory.			✓
• Salary of worker assembling the planes.		✓	

9 TRIP LTD

Cost	Materials	Labour	Overheads
• Wages of the insurance clerks dealing with claims.		✓	
• Rent of the office.			✓
• Paper used to print off insurance policies.	✓		
• Salary of the office manager.		✓	

10 FRUWT LTD

Cost	Materials	Labour	Overheads
• Purchase of fruit for juicing.	✓		
• Electricity used by juicing machines.			✓
• Water added to the juice before sale.	✓		
• Wages of staff operating juicing machinery.		✓	

11   MARTIN

Cost	Materials	Labour	Overheads
• Stationery used in Martin's court cases.	✓		
• Wages of Martin's secretary.		✓	
• Water rates for Martin's office.			✓
• Cost of training courses taken by Martin.			✓

CLASSIFYING COSTS BY NATURE (DIRECT OR INDIRECT)

12   RUSSELL

Cost	Direct	Indirect
• Paper used in the newspapers.	✓	
• Wages of warehouse staff.		✓
• Heat and light for head office.		✓
• Ink used in printing the newspapers.	✓	

13   RUSSETT LTD

Cost	Direct	Indirect
• Glass used to make tablets.	✓	
• Insurance of factory.		✓
• Wages of workers assembling tablets.	✓	
• Cost of entertaining corporate clients.		✓

14   SCOTLAND LTD

Cost	Direct	Indirect
• Cleaners' wages.		✓
• Advertising expense.		✓
• Material used in production.	✓	
• Production manager's wages.		✓
• Machinist wages.	✓	

15   DIRECT OR INDIRECT

Cost	Direct	Indirect
• Chargeable hour for a lawyer.	✓	
• Machine hire for a building contractor in a long term contract.	✓	
• Electricity for a garden centre.		✓
• Audit fee for a restaurant.		✓

16 DIRECT COSTS

B

Direct costs are variable and are therefore usually assumed to be constant, regardless of the level of activity within the relevant range. Answer A is incorrect because it describes the behaviour of a fixed cost within the relevant range of activity. Answer C also describes a fixed cost, since the same total fixed cost would be shared over a varying number of units, resulting in a unit cost that varies with changes in activity levels. Answer D is incorrect because total variable costs are conventionally deemed to remain unaltered when activity levels remain constant.

CLASSIFYING COSTS BY FUNCTION (PRODUCTION, ADMINISTRATION OR SELLING AND DISTRIBUTION)

17 NOOGLE LTD

Cost	Production	Administration	Selling and distribution
• Purchases of plastic for ready meal containers.	✓		
• Depreciation of sales department's delivery lorries.			✓
• Insurance of office computers.		✓	
• Salaries of production workers.	✓		

18 HEAVING LTD

Cost	Production	Administration	Selling and distribution
• Paper used to print off sales invoices.		✓	
• Metal used to make weights and bars.	✓		
• Depreciation of sales person's vehicle.			✓
• Repairs to machine in factory.	✓		

19 KORMA PLC

Cost	Production	Administration	Selling and distribution	Finance
• Direct materials.	✓			
• Sales director's salary.			✓	
• Head office printer ink.		✓		
• Direct labour.	✓			
• Bank charges.				✓

20 JAMES

Cost	Production	Administration	Selling and distribution	Finance
• Salary of receptionist.		✓		
• Plastic used in false teeth.	✓			
• Stationery provided to all departments.		✓		
• Interest on James' bank overdraft.				✓
• Electricity for James' factory.	✓			

CLASSIFYING COSTS BY BEHAVIOUR (FIXED, VARIABLE OR SEMI-VARIABLE)

21 QUARK LTD

Cost	Fixed	Variable	Semi-variable
• Bar manager's salary.	✓		
• Alcohol used to make drinks.		✓	
• Rent of bar.	✓		
• Telephone costs, including standard line rental charge.			✓

22 MORN LTD

Cost	Fixed	Variable	Semi-variable
• Wood used in production.		✓	
• Advertising manager's salary.	✓		
• Electricity costs which include a standing charge.			✓
• Labour costs paid on a piecework basis.		✓	

23 STEPPED FIXED COST

A

A supervisor's wages are usually classified as a step cost because a supervisor may be responsible for supervising up to a specific number of workers. However, if output increases such that additional direct labour is required, then an extra supervisor will be required.

| 1 – 10 workers | 1 supervisor |
| 11 – 20 workers | 2 supervisors |

24 BRAETAK LTD

Cost	Fixed	Variable	Semi-variable
• Rent of an office building.	✓		
• Wages of production staff paid on an hourly basis.		✓	
• Wages of production staff paid by a piece rate method.		✓	
• Sales staff paid a basic wage plus commission for each unit sold.			✓

Note: the piece rate scheme does not mention a guaranteed minimum wage so the correct answer is variable.

25 ODO LTD

Cost	Fixed	Variable	Semi-variable
• Material used in the production process.		✓	
• Safety review fee for the year.	✓		
• Electricity costs which include a standing charge.			✓
• Labour paid on a per unit basis.		✓	

26 DEFINITIONS

Behaviour	Fixed	Variable	Semi-variable	Stepped cost
• This type of cost increases in direct proportion to the amount of units produced.		✓		
• This type of cost has a fixed and a variable element.			✓	
• This type of cost remains constant despite changes in output.	✓			
• This type of cost is fixed within a certain range of output.				✓

27 MATCH A GRAPH

(a) Variable cost per unit – graph 1

(b) Total fixed cost – graph 1

(c) Stepped fixed costs – graph 3

(d) Total variable cost – graph 2

(e) Semi-variable cost – graph 4

COST CODING

28 BYTES LTD

Cost	Code
• Salary of trainee IT consultant.	• B100
• Planning costs to renew lease of the office.	• C200
• Wages of the office manager.	• B200
• Cleaning materials used by cleaner.	• A200

29 HERO LTD

Transaction	Code
• Cost of major advertising campaign.	• 760/340
• Oil for machine in factory.	• 225/115
• Silk used in manufacturing of costumes.	• 225/110
• Insurance of head office.	• 485/230
• Sale of women's costumes to a supermarket chain.	• 115/085
• Wages paid to delivery van drivers.	• 760/340

30 VILLAIN LTD

Transaction	Code
• Petrol used to run drilling machinery.	• 015/200
• Sale of silver to a jewellery manufacturer.	• 011/200
• Replacement of worn out drilling machinery parts.	• 015/200
• Depreciation of fleet of delivery lorries.	• 024/200
• Salary of finance director.	• 019/200
• Sale of gold to an electronics company.	• 011/100

31   NAYULZ LTD

Cost	Code
• Income earned from salons in New York City, America.	RE228
• Bank loans raised to open a new store in London.	IN100
• Nail polish purchased for use in salon.	CO315
• Heat and light for salon.	CO325
• Nayulz funds invested in new project.	IN110

32   JUMPER LTD

Sale	Code
• Sale of one jumper to Mrs S. Wooley.	KNI/315
• Sale of protective trousers to a factory in London.	TRS/635
• Sale of large coats to an office in Birmingham.	MCN/515
• Sale of woolen jumpers to a shop in Halifax.	KNI/425
• Sale of four coats to Mr A. West.	MCN/315
• Sale of three hundred trousers to a shop in Manchester.	TRS/425

33   GREENFINGERS

Cost	Code
• Purchase of seeds used to grow plants for resale.	CS880
• External loans for investment in new greenhouses.	IN515
• Wages of gardeners who maintain the plants to be sold.	CS890
• Sales of food and drink.	RV795

COST BEHAVIOUR

CALCULATION QUESTIONS

34   HULK PLC

Statement	Fixed	Variable	Semi-variable
• Costs are £37,500 when 7,500 units are made and £62,500 when 12,500 units are made.		✓	
• Costs are £2 per unit when 7,500 units are made and £1.20 per unit when 12,500 units are made.	✓		
• Costs are £50,000 when 7,500 units are made and £80,000 when 12,500 units are made.			✓

35   BANNER PLC

Statement	Fixed	Variable	Semi-variable
• Costs are £5,000 plus £45 per unit, regardless of the number of units made.			✓
• Costs are £5,000 when 300 units are made and £5,000 when 600 units are made.	✓		
• Costs are £35 per unit regardless of the number of units made.		✓	

36   NORTON PLC

Statement	Fixed	Variable	Semi-variable
• Costs are £50,000 in total regardless of the number of units made.	✓		
• Costs are £50,000 in total when 2,500 units are made and £80,000 when 4,000 units are made.		✓	
• Costs are £7 per unit when 1,000 units are made and £6 per unit when 2,000 units are made.			✓

Note: The third cost must be semi-variable as it cannot be fixed (it changes as the number of units changes) and it cannot be purely variable as the cost per unit changes at different levels of activity.

37   TRIUMPH LTD

Task 1

Statement	Fixed	Variable	Semi-variable
At 9,000 units this cost is £29,250, and at 12,000 units it is £39,000		✓	
At 5,000 units this cost is £5.20 per unit, and at 8,000 units it is £3.25 per unit	✓		
At 19,800 units, this cost is £64,500, and at 27,000 units it is £82,500			✓

£29,250 ÷ 9,000 units = £3.25, £39,000 ÷ 12,000 units = £3.25, therefore variable cost

5,000 units × £5.20 = £26,000, 8,000 units × £3.25 = £26,000, therefore fixed cost

£64,500 ÷ 19,800 units = £3.26, £82,500 ÷ 27,000 units = £3.06, therefore must be a **semi-variable** cost – it cannot be fixed (it changes as the number of units changes) and it cannot be purely variable as the cost per unit changes at different levels of activity.

Task 2

	6,000 units	7,000 units	10,000 units	14,000 units
Variable cost (£)	18,000			42,000
Fixed cost (£)	24,000			24,000
Total cost (£)	42,000	45,000	54,000	66,000

Using the hi-lo method:

For the volumes given, difference in costs = 54,000 − 45,000 = £9,000

Difference in volumes = 10,000 − 7,000 = 3,000 units

Therefore variable cost per unit = £9,000 ÷ 3,000 units = £3/unit

At 10,000 units, fixed costs = £54,000 − (10,000 × £3) = £24,000

38 YOUNGS LTD

Task 1

Statement	Fixed	Variable	Semi-variable
At 4,000 units this cost is £3.00 per unit, and at 6,000 units it is £2.00 per unit.	✓		
At 7,000 units this cost is £32,500, and at 10,000 units it is £43,000.			✓
At 11,000 units this cost is £57,750, and at 15,000 units it is £78,750.		✓	

4,000 units × £3.00 = £12,000, 6,000 units × £2.00 = £12,000, therefore **fixed** cost

£32,500 ÷ 7,000 units = £4.64, £43,000 ÷ 10,000 units = £4.30, therefore must be a **semi-variable** cost – it cannot be fixed (it changes as the number of units changes) and it cannot be purely variable as the cost per unit changes at different levels of activity.

£57,750 ÷ 11,000 units = £5.25, £78,750 ÷ 15,000 units = £5.25, therefore **variable** cost

Task 2

	8,000 units	10,000 units	13,000 units	16,000 units
Variable cost (£)	34,000			68,000
Fixed cost (£)	18,000			18,000
Total cost (£)	52,000	60,500	73,250	86,000

Using the hi-lo method:

For the volumes given, difference in costs = 73,250 – 60,500 = £12,750

Difference in volumes = 13,000 – 10,000 = 3,000 units

Therefore variable cost per unit = £12,750 ÷ 3,000 units = £4.25/unit

At 10,000 units, fixed costs = £60,500 – (10,000 × £4.25) = £18,000

39   CARE PLC

Task 1

Statement	Fixed	Variable	Semi-variable
At 8,000 units this cost is £38,000, and at 12,000 units it is £49,000			✓
At 10,500 units this cost is £39,375, and at 14,000 units it is £52,500		✓	
At 4,000 units this cost is £4.50 per unit, and at 6,000 units is £3.00 per unit	✓		

£38,000 ÷ 8,000 units = £4.75, £49,000 ÷ 12,000 units = £4.08, therefore must be a **semi-variable** cost – it cannot be fixed (it changes as the number of units changes) and it cannot be purely variable as the cost per unit changes at different levels of activity.

£39,375 ÷ 10,500 units = £3.75, £52,500 ÷ 14,000 units = £3.75, therefore **variable** cost

4,000 units × £4.50 = £18,000, 6,000 units × £3.00 = £18,000, therefore **fixed** cost

Task 2

	3,000 units	5,000 units	9,000 units	12,000 units
Variable cost (£)	5,100			20,400
Fixed cost (£)	4,500			4,500
Total cost (£)	9,600	13,000	19,800	24,900

Using the hi-lo method:

For the volumes given, difference in costs = 19,800 – 13,000 = £6,800

Difference in volumes = 9,000 – 5,000 = 4,000 units

Therefore variable cost per unit = £6,800 ÷ 4,000 units = £1.70/unit

At 9,000 units, fixed costs = £19,800 – (9,000 × £1.70) = £4,500

40   ROBSHAW LTD

Task 1

Statement	Fixed	Variable	Semi-variable
At 6,000 units this cost is £3.75 per unit, and at 9,000 units it is £2.50 per unit	✓		
At 8,500 units this cost is £36,550, and at 11,300 units it is £48,590		✓	
At 11,000 units this cost is £27,750, and at 14,000 units it is £33,000			✓

6,000 units × £3.75 = £22,500, 9,000 units × £2.50 = £22,500, therefore **fixed** cost

£36,550 ÷ 8,500 units = £4.30, £48,590 ÷ 11,300 units = £4.30, therefore **variable** cost

£27,750 ÷ 11,000 units = £2.52, £33,000 ÷ 14,000 units = £2.36, therefore must be a **semi-variable** cost – it cannot be fixed (it changes as the number of units changes) and it cannot be purely variable as the cost per unit changes at different levels of activity.

Task 2

	9,000 units	11,000 units	14,000 units	16,500 units
Variable cost (£)	29,250			53,625
Fixed cost (£)	4,500			4,500
Total cost (£)	33,750	40,250	50,000	58,125

Using the hi-lo method:

For the volumes given, difference in costs = 50,000 – 40,250 = £9,750

Difference in volumes = 14,000 – 11,000 = 3,000 units

Therefore variable cost per unit = £9,750 ÷ 3,000 units = £3.25/unit

At 11,000 units, fixed costs = £40,250 – (11,000 × £3.25) = £4,500

NARRATIVE STYLE QUESTIONS

41 BUNGLE LTD

Statement	True	False
• Total variable costs will decrease.		✓
• Total fixed costs will remain the same.	✓	
• The variable cost per unit will remain the same.	✓	
• The fixed cost per unit will increase.		✓

42 TF

Statement	True	False
• Variable costs change directly with changes in activity.	✓	
• Fixed costs change directly with changes in activity.		✓
• Stepped costs are fixed within a set range of output.	✓	

43 FIXED OR VARIABLE

Cost	Fixed	Variable
• Direct materials.		✓
• Power used in production machinery.		✓
• Training costs for new employees in production.	✓	
• Insurance for sales cars.	✓	
• Insurance machinery.	✓	
• Sales commission.		✓

44 FOV

Cost	Fixed	Variable
• Piecework wages paid to factory workers.		✓
• Salaries paid to company directors.	✓	
• Annual payment for cleaning of air conditioning units.	✓	

45 VOF

Cost	Fixed	Variable
• Annual salaries paid to factory managers.	✓	
• Hourly wages paid to factory workers.		✓
• Colour ink used to print magazines.		✓

46 STORM

	Overhead?	
Cost	Yes	No
• Labour cost of workers who assemble the product.		✓
• Insurance cost of factory where product is assembled.	✓	
• Heat and light for manufacturing machines.	✓	

47 ROGUE

	Overhead?	
Cost	Yes	No
• Labour cost of cleaning staff in a factory.	✓	
• Depreciation of delivery vans.	✓	
• Cost of materials used to build the product.		✓

48 GAMBIT

	Overhead?	
Cost	Yes	No
• Wages of staff paid on a piecework system.		✓
• Cost of factory canteen staff hourly wages.	✓	
• Direct materials.		✓

COST CARDS, TOTAL COSTS AND UNIT COSTS

49   JEEPERS LTD

Cost	Yes	No
• Materials used in production.	✓	
• Piecework labour costs.	✓	
• Salary of chief executive.		✓

Element	Unit product cost
Materials	£35
Labour	£8
Direct cost	£43
Overheads	£38
Total	£81

50   BRANIAC LTD

Element	Unit cost
Materials	£24.50
Labour	£40.25
Direct cost	£64.75
Overheads	£12.50
Total	£77.25

51   GLORIA LTD

Element	Unit cost	Total cost for 20,000 units
Variable production costs	£5.50	£110,000
Fixed production costs	£4.00	£80,000
Total production cost	£9.50	£190,000

52   BIZARRO LTD

Element	Unit cost	Total cost
Materials	£45.00	£765,000
Labour	£9.00	£153,000
Overheads	£2.50	£42,500
Total	£56.50	£960,500

53   VINNY LTD

Element	Unit cost	Total cost
Materials	£5.00	£100,000
Labour	£8.00	£160,000
Overheads	£5.00	£100,000
Total	£18.00	£360,000

54   DARKSEID LTD

Element	Unit cost
Materials	£3.50
Labour	£6.75
Fixed overheads	£2.42
Total	£12.67

55   DOOMSDAY LTD

Element	Total cost for 20,000 units	Unit cost
Direct costs	£1,250,000	£62.50
Production overhead	£75,000	£3.75
Non production overhead	£185,000	£9.25
Total costs	£1,510,000	£75.50

56   OLSEN LTD

Element	Total cost	Unit cost
Materials	£960,000	£12.00
Labour	£1,360,000	£17.00
Production overheads	£80,000	£1.00
Administration overheads	£40,000	£0.50
Total	£2,440,000	£30.50

57   FLAKEWAY LTD

Element	Unit cost
Materials	£5.00
Labour	£4.00
Fixed overheads	£2.00
Total	£11.00

58   CORONATION LTD

	Total cost for 5,000 units	Unit cost
Direct costs	£32,500	£6.50
Production overhead	£40,000	£8.00
Non production overhead	£45,000	£9.00
Total costs	£117,500	£23.50

59   LUTHOR LTD

Element	Unit cost
Materials	£60.00
Labour	£22.50
Fixed overheads	£38.00
Total	£120.50

60   WILKINSON LTD

Task 1

	Machine hour	Labour hour	Unit
Overheads (£)	150,000	150,000	150,000
Activity	10,000	12,500	60,000
Absorption rate (£)	15.00	12.00	2.50

Task 2

Cost	Machine hour (£)	Labour hour (£)	Unit (£)
Material	10.00	10.00	10.00
Labour	2.50	2.50	2.50
Direct cost	12.50	12.50	12.50
Overheads	2.50	3.00	2.50
Total unit cost	15.00	15.50	15.00

61   HODGSON LTD

Task 1

	Machine hour	Labour hour	Unit
Overheads (£)	250,000	250,000	250,000
Activity	15,000	20,000	100,000
Absorption rate (£)	16.67	12.50	2.50

Task 2

Cost	Machine hour (£)	Labour hour (£)	Unit (£)
Material	24.00	24.00	24.00
Labour	6.00	6.00	6.00
Direct cost	30.00	30.00	30.00
Overheads	5.56	6.25	2.50
Total unit cost	35.56	36.25	32.50

62 BARNES LTD

Task 1

	Machine hour	Labour hour	Unit
Overheads (£)	130,000	130,000	130,000
Activity	17,500	12,000	40,000
Absorption rate (£)	7.43	10.83	3.25

Task 2

Cost	Machine hour (£)	Labour hour (£)	Unit (£)
Material	15.00	15.00	15.00
Labour	5.00	5.00	5.00
Direct cost	20.00	20.00	20.00
Overheads	3.72	3.61	3.25
Total unit cost	23.72	23.61	23.25

63 ANDREW LTD

Task 1

	Machine hour	Labour hour	Unit
Overheads (£)	145,000	145,000	145,000
Activity	9,000	11,000	60,000
Absorption rate (£)	16.11	13.18	2.42

Task 2

Cost	Machine hour (£)	Labour hour (£)	Unit (£)
Material	8.00	8.00	8.00
Labour	7.00	7.00	7.00
Direct cost	15.00	15.00	15.00
Overheads	5.37	6.59	2.42
Total unit cost	20.37	21.59	17.42

MANUFACTURING ACCOUNTS

64   JOKER LTD

Manufacturing account – Y/E 31 December

	£
Opening inventory of raw materials	50,000
Purchases of raw materials	120,000
Closing inventory of raw materials	65,000
DIRECT MATERIALS USED	
Direct labour	140,000
DIRECT COST	
Manufacturing overheads	85,000
MANUFACTURING COST	
Opening inventory of work in progress	48,000
Closing inventory of work in progress	52,000
COST OF GOODS MANUFACTURED	
Opening inventory of finished goods	57,000
Closing inventory of finished goods	61,000
COST OF GOODS SOLD	

	£
DIRECT MATERIALS USED	105,000
DIRECT COST	245,000
MANUFACTURING COST	330,000
COST OF GOODS MANUFACTURED	326,000
COST OF GOODS SOLD	322,000

65   TUT LTD

Manufacturing account – Y/E 31 July

	£
Opening inventory of raw materials	10,000
Purchases of raw materials	60,000
Closing inventory of raw materials	12,000
DIRECT MATERIALS USED	58,000
Direct labour	88,000
DIRECT COST	146,000
Manufacturing overheads	45,000
MANUFACTURING COST	191,000
Opening inventory of work in progress	12,000
Closing inventory of work in progress	15,000
COST OF GOODS MANUFACTURED	188,000
Opening inventory of finished goods	18,000
Closing inventory of finished goods	20,000
COST OF GOODS SOLD	186,000

	£
DIRECT MATERIALS USED	58,000
DIRECT COST	146,000
MANUFACTURING COST	191,000
COST OF GOODS MANUFACTURED	188,000
COST OF GOODS SOLD	186,000

66   RIDDLER LTD

Manufacturing account – Y/E 31 May

	£
Opening inventory of raw materials	14,000
Purchases of raw materials	100,000
Closing inventory of raw materials	20,000
DIRECT MATERIALS USED	94,000
Direct labour	194,000
DIRECT COST	288,000
Manufacturing overheads	106,000
MANUFACTURING COST	394,000
Opening inventory of work in progress	16,000
Closing inventory of work in progress	20,000
COST OF GOODS MANUFACTURED	390,000
Opening inventory of finished goods	60,000
Closing inventory of finished goods	50,000
COST OF GOODS SOLD	400,000

67   CLOCKING LTD

Manufacturing account – Y/E 31 May

	£
Opening inventory of raw materials	7,000
Purchases of raw materials	50,000
Closing inventory of raw materials	10,000
DIRECT MATERIALS USED	47,000
Direct labour	97,000
DIRECT COST	144,000
Manufacturing overheads	53,000
MANUFACTURING COST	197,000
Opening inventory of work in progress	8,000
Closing of work in progress	10,000
COST OF GOODS MANUFACTURED	195,000
Opening inventory of finished goods	30,000
Closing inventory of finished goods	25,000
COST OF GOODS SOLD	200,000

68   BOOKWORM LTD

Manufacturing account – Y/E 31 December

	£
Opening inventory of raw materials	5,000
Purchases of raw materials	15,000
Closing inventory of raw materials	8,000
DIRECT MATERIALS USED	**12,000**
Direct labour	15,000
DIRECT COST	**27,000**
Manufacturing overheads	25,000
MANUFACTURING COST	**52,000**
Opening inventory of work in progress	4,000
Closing inventory of work in progress	(6,000)
COST OF GOODS MANUFACTURED	**50,000**
Opening inventory of finished goods	12,000
Closing inventory of finished goods	(16,000)
COST OF GOODS SOLD	**46,000**

69   MULTI

C – Manufacturing cost + opening WIP – closing WIP + opening FG – closing FG

COSTING FOR INVENTORY AND WORK-IN-PROGRESS

NARRATIVE STYLE QUESTIONS

70   BOBBLE LTD

Characteristic	FIFO	LIFO	AVCO
• Potentially out of date valuation of inventory issues.	✓		
• The valuation of inventory rarely reflects the actual purchase price of the material.			✓
• Potentially out of date closing inventory valuation.		✓	

71 LINT LTD

Statement	True	False
• In periods of rising prices, FIFO gives a higher valuation of closing inventory than LIFO or AVCO.	✓	
• In periods of falling prices, LIFO gives a higher valuation of issues of inventory than FIFO or AVCO.		✓
• AVCO would normally be expected to produce a valuation of closing inventory somewhere between valuations under FIFO and LIFO.	✓	

72 FLUFF LTD

Characteristic	FIFO	LIFO	AVCO
• This inventory valuation method is particularly suited to inventory that consist of liquid materials e.g. oil.			✓
• This inventory valuation method is suited to inventory that has a short shelf life e.g. dairy products.	✓		
• This inventory valuation method is suited to a wheat farmer who has large silos of grain. Grain is added to and taken from the top of these silos.		✓	

73 FIDO LTD

Characteristic	FIFO	LIFO	AVCO
• In times of rising prices this method will give higher profits.	✓		
• In times of rising prices this method will give lower profits.		✓	
• In times of rising prices this method gives a middle level of profits compared to the other two.			✓

74 TRUFFEAUX LTD

Statement	True	False
• FIFO costs issues of inventory at the most recent purchase price.		✓
• AVCO costs issues of inventory at the oldest purchase price.		✓
• LIFO costs issues of inventory at the oldest purchase price.		✓
• FIFO values closing inventory at the most recent purchase price.	✓	
• LIFO values closing inventory at the most recent purchase price.		✓
• AVCO values closing inventory at the latest purchase price.		✓

75 STOCKY LTD

Characteristic	FIFO	LIFO	AVCO
• Issues are valued at the most recent purchase cost.		✓	
• Inventory is valued at the average of the cost of purchases.			✓
• Inventory is valued at the most recent purchase cost.	✓		

IDENTIFICATION OF INVENTORY VALUATION METHOD

76 EPIC LTD

Task 1

Characteristic	FIFO	LIFO	AVCO
• Closing inventory is valued at £28,200.			✓
• The issue of inventory is valued at £67,000.	✓		
• The issue of inventory is valued at £64,000.		✓	

Task 2

	True	False
• AVCO values the issue of inventory at £65,800.	✓	
• LIFO values the closing inventory at £27,000.		✓
• FIFO values the closing inventory at £30,000.		✓

77 AWESOME LTD

Task 1

Characteristic	FIFO	LIFO	AVCO
• Closing inventory is valued at £48,500.	✓		
• The issue of inventory is valued at £57,200.			✓
• The issue of inventory is valued at £66,900.		✓	

Task 2

	True	False
• FIFO values the issue of inventory at £47,500.	✓	
• AVCO values the closing inventory at £38,400.		✓
• LIFO values the closing inventory at £29,100.	✓	

78 AMAZING LTD

Task 1

Characteristic	FIFO	LIFO	AVCO
• Closing inventory is valued at £1,500.		✓	
• The issue of inventory is valued at £23,000.	✓		
• The issue of inventory is valued at £24,000.			✓

Task 2

	True	False
• LIFO values the issue of inventory at £26,500.	✓	
• AVCO values the closing inventory at £5,000.		✓
• FIFO values the closing inventory at £4,000.		✓

INVENTORY CARDS

79 STONE LTD

Method	Cost of issue on 22 June	Closing inventory at 30 June
FIFO	£10,125 (500 × £15) + (150 × £17.50)	£17,200 (£8,750 + £4,950 + £6,125 + £7,500) − £10,125
LIFO	£11,450 (275 × £18) + (350 × £17.50) + (25 × £15)	£15,875 (£8,750 + £4,950 + £6,125 + £7,500) − £11,450
AVCO	£10,732 ((£7,500 + £6,125 + £4,950)/ (500 + 350 + 275)) × 650	£16,593 (£8,750 + £4,950 + £6,125 + £7,500) − £10,732

80 NATAL LTD

Task 1

Method	Cost of issue on 2 Dec	Closing inventory at 29 Dec
LIFO	£534,250 (50,000 × £7) + (14,000 × £8) + (8500 × £8.50)	£42,750 (£85,000 + £112,000 + £350,000 + £30,000) − £534,250
AVCO	£535,912 ((£85,000 + £112,000 + £350,000)/ (10,000 + 14,000 + 50,000)) × 72,500	£41,088 (£85,000 + £112,000 + £350,000 + £30,000) − £535,912

Task 2

	True	False
• FIFO would give a lower closing inventory valuation on the 29th December than LIFO and AVCO.	✓	
• FIFO would give a lower cost of issue on the 25th of December than LIFO and AVCO.		✓

81   GANDALF LTD

	Valuation £
• July 15	£1,030 **(500 × £1.70) + (120 × £1.50)**
• July 31	£660 **(200 × £1.80) + (200 × £1.50)**

360 + 300

82   GRUNDY LTD

Method	Cost of issue on 25 October	Closing inventory at 31 October
FIFO	£20,000 **(6000 × £2.50) + (2500 × £2)**	£5,500
LIFO	£15,250 **(3000 × £1) + (3000 × £2) + (2500 × £2.50)**	£10,250
AVCO	£17,000 **(AVCO = £24,000/12000 units = £2/unit** **Cost of issue = 8500 × £2)**	£8,500

Tutorial note

The quickest way to calculate closing inventory is as total purchases (£25,500) less cost of issues.

83   LOBO LTD

Method	Cost of issue on 29 May	Closing inventory at 30 May
FIFO	£2,500 **(250 × £5.50) + (250 × £4.50)**	£2,250
LIFO	£1,000 **(500 × £2)**	£3,750
AVCO	£1,750 **(AVCO = £4,375/1,250 = £3.50/unit, giving cost of issue of 500 × £3.50)**	£3,000

Tutorial note

Quickest to calculate closing inventory as total purchases (£4,750) less cost of issue

84   ZOD LTD

Tutorial note

This question is harder than those seen in the sample assessment but is here to give you more of a challenge!

Method	Cost of issue on 16 Feb	Closing inventory at 26 Feb
FIFO	£290	£905
AVCO (see working below)	£255	£924

AVCO Workings:

DATE	RECEIPTS		ISSUES		BALANCE		
	Units	Cost	Units	Cost	Units	Unit cost	Total cost
February 2	100	£500			100	£5	£500
February 3			50		**(50)**	**(£5)**	**(£250)**
					50	£5	£250
February 12	150	£600			**150**	**£4**	**£600**
					200	£4.25	£850
February 16			60		**(60)**	**(£4.25)**	**(£255)**
					140	(£4.25)	£595
February 20	110	£505			**110**	£4.59 (to nearest penny)	**£505**
					250	£4.40	£1,100
February 26			40		**(40)**	**(£4.40)**	**(£176)**
					210	4.40	£924

COSTING FOR LABOUR

NARRATIVE STYLE QUESTIONS

85   NULAB LTD

Payment method	Time-rate	Piecework	Piece-rate plus bonus
• Labour is paid based on the production achieved.		✓	
• Labour is paid extra if an agreed level of output is exceeded.			✓
• Labour is paid according to hours worked.	✓		

86   LU LTD

Payment method	Time-rate	Piecework	Time-rate plus bonus
• Assured level of remuneration for employee.	✓		
• Employee earns more if they work more efficiently than expected.		✓	
• Assured level of remuneration and reward for working efficiently.			✓

87   MANDELA LTD

Statement	True	False
• Time rate is paid based on the production achieved.		✓
• Overtime is paid for hours worked over the standard hours agreed.	✓	
• Piece rate is paid according to hours worked.		✓

88   PERRES LTD

Payment method	Basic rate	Overtime premium	Overtime rate
• This is the amount paid above the basic rate for hours worked in excess of the normal hours.		✓	
• This is the total amount paid per hour for hours worked in excess of the normal hours.			✓
• This is the amount paid per hour for normal hours worked.	✓		

89 TEVEZ LTD

Statement	True	False
• Direct labour costs can be identified with the goods being made or the service being provided.	✓	
• Indirect labour costs vary directly with the level of activity.		✓

90 BERDYCH LTD

Payment method	Variable	Fixed
• Labour that is paid based on a time rate basis per hour worked.	✓	
• Labour is paid on a monthly salary basis.		✓
• Labour that is based on number of units produced.	✓	

91 SODERLING LTD

Payment method	Time-rate	Piecework	Salary
• Assured level of remuneration for employee usually agreed for the year.			✓
• Employee earnings are directly linked with units they produce.		✓	
• Employee earnings are directly linked with hours they work.	✓		

92 MURRAY LTD

	True	False
• Indirect labour costs includes production supervisors' salaries.	✓	
• Direct labour costs usually vary directly with the level of activity.	✓	

93 OWEN LTD

Payment method	Time-rate	Piecework	Salary
• Employee is paid the same amount every month.			✓
• Employee wage increases in direct correlation with the number of hours worked.	✓		
• Employee wage increases in direct correlation with the number of units produced.		✓	

94   PIECEWORK STATEMENTS

Statement	True	False
• Piecework encourages employees to work harder.	✓	
• Piecework requires accurate recording of the number of hours staff have worked.		✓
• Piecework encourages workers to improve the quality of the units they produce.		✓

CALCULATING LABOUR COSTS

95   MUTANT LTD

Worker	Hours worked	Basic wage	Overtime	Gross wage
S. Torm	34 hours	£240	£23	£263
J. Grey	38 hours	£240	£68	£308

96   PHOENIX LTD

Statement	True	False
An employee who works 38 hours and makes 775 units will not receive a bonus.		✓
An employee who works 40 hours and makes 815 units will receive total pay of £342.50.	✓	
An employee who works 37 hours and makes 744 units will earn a bonus of £6.	✓	

97   KAHN LTD

Worker	Hours worked	Units produced	Basic wage	Bonus	Gross wage
A. Smith	35	175	£420	£0	£420
J. O'Hara	35	180	£420	£6	£426
M.Stizgt	35	185	£420	£12	£432

98   ENTERPRISE LTD

Worker	Hours worked	Basic wage	Overtime	Gross wage
J. Picard	37 hours	£420	£36	£456
B. Crusher	42 hours	£420	£126	£546
D. Troi	31 hours	£372	£0	£372

99   SGC LTD

Worker	Units produced in week	Gross wage
J. O'Neill	500 units	£660.00
S. Carter	650 units	£772.50

100   GOTHIC LTD

Worker	Hours worked	Units produced	Basic wage	Bonus	Gross wage
M. Shelley	37	300	£629	£20	£649
G. Leroux	37	312	£629	£80	£709
E. A. Poe	37	296	£629	£0	£629

101   AVENGERS LTD

Worker	Hours worked	Basic wage	Overtime	Gross wage
T. Stark	138	£1,380	£0	£1,380
B. Banner	142	£1,400	£25	£1,425
S. Rogers	145	£1,400	£63	£1,463

102   DRACO LTD

Worker	Units produced in week	Gross wage
P. Jones	240 units	£192
D. Bannatyne	350 units	£250
L. Redford	250 units	£200

103   QUAGGA PLC

Statement	True	False
During a 29 hour week, an employee producing 1,475 units would not receive a bonus.		✓
During a 32 hour week, an employee producing 1,665 units would receive a bonus of £29.25.	✓	
During a 37 hour week, an employee producing 1,925 units would receive total pay of £300.25.		✓

104 JLA PLC

Statement	True	False
During a 30 hour week, an employee producing 192 units would receive a bonus of £16.	✓	
During a 35 hour week, an employee producing 240 units would receive total pay of £215.	✓	
During a 30 hour week, an employee producing 180 units would not receive a bonus.	✓	

105 INJUSTICE LTD

Worker	Units produced	Basic wage	Piece work	Gross wage
N. Wing	295	£175	£354	£529
W. Woman	355	£175	£426	£601
T. Flash	385	£175	£462	£637

106 GREENWOOD LTD

Worker	Hours worked	Units produced	Basic wage	Bonus	Gross wage
B. Ryan	35	175	£350	£0	£350
S. Chang	35	190	£350	£21	£371
E. Schneider	35	210	£350	£49	£399

VARIANCES

NARRATIVE QUESTIONS

107 VARIOUS LTD

Statement	True	False
• A variance is the difference between budgeted and actual cost.	✓	
• A favourable variance means actual costs are less than budgeted.	✓	
• An adverse variance means that actual income is less than budgeted.	✓	
• A favourable variance occurs when actual income is the same as budgeted income.		✓

108 JONES LTD

Statement	True	False
If budgeted sales are 6,000 units at £7.50 per unit and actual sales are £47,600, the sales variance is favourable	✓	
A favourable cost variance occurs when an actual cost of £9,800 is compared to a budgeted cost of £24 per unit for a budgeted output of 400 units		✓
A variance arises from a comparison of budgeted costs for last year with actual costs for this year		✓
If actual material costs are the same as budgeted costs for materials then no variance arises	✓	

109 GATLAND LTD

Statement	True	False
If budgeted sales are 4,000 units at £9.50 per unit and actual sales are £35,200, the sales variance is favourable		✓
A favourable cost variance occurs when an actual cost of £6,400 is compared to a budgeted cost of £14 per unit for a budgeted output of 500 units	✓	
A variance arises from a comparison of budgeted costs for last year with budgeted costs for this year		✓
If actual material costs are the same as budgeted costs for materials then the materials variance is adverse		✓

110 LANCASTER LTD

Statement	True	False
If budgeted sales are 14,000 units at £3.50 per unit and actual sales are £45,200, the sales variance is favourable		✓
An adverse cost variance occurs when an actual cost of £68,400 is compared to a budgeted cost of £14 per unit for a budgeted output of 5,000 units		✓
A variance arises from a comparison of budgeted costs for this year with actual costs for this year	✓	
If actual material costs are the same as budgeted costs for materials then the materials variance is favourable		✓

111 GOODE LTD

Statement	True	False
The variance for the Direct Material cost of Department B should be reported to the purchasing manager	✓	
The variance for the Direct Labour cost for Department A should be reported to the sales manager		✓
The variance for the Direct Labour cost for Department B should be reported to the production manager of Department A		✓
A Direct Material cost variance that has been deemed Not Significant should not be reported	✓	

112 BROWN LTD

Statement	True	False
The variance for the Direct Material cost of Department A should be reported to the purchasing manager	✓	
The variance for the Direct Labour cost for Department A should be reported to the production manager of Department B		✓
The variance for sales should be reported to the sales manager	✓	
A Direct Material cost variance that has been deemed Significant should not be reported		✓

VARIANCE CALCULATION QUESTIONS

113 EREBOR LTD

Cost type	Budget £	Actual £	Variance £	Adverse or favourable (A or F)
Sales	600,500	597,800	2,700	A
Direct materials	205,800	208,500	2,700	A
Direct labour	155,000	154,800	200	F
Production overheads	65,000	72,100	7,100	A
Administration overheads	58,400	55,200	3,200	F

114 MORIA LTD

Cost type	Budget	Variance	Variance as % of budget	Significant or Not significant
Sales	45,100	4,214	9	S
Material	15,750	1,260	8	S
Labour	12,915	805	6	NS
Variable overheads	5,750	315	5	NS
Fixed overheads	8,155	1,011	12	S

115 WYEDALE LTD

Cost type	Budget £	Actual £	Variance £	Variance %	Adverse/ Favourable
Sales	27,000	29,775	2,775	10	F
Direct materials	7,400	8,510	1,110	15	A
Direct labour	7,200	7,920	720	10	A
Production overheads	5,500	5,390	110	2	F
Administration overheads	4,500	4,365	135	3	F

116 BELEGOST LTD

	Budget £	Actual £	Adverse or Favourable (A or F)	Significant or Not significant (S or NS)
Sales	205,000	207,100	F	NS
Direct materials	75,150	78,750	A	NS
Direct labour	110,556	107,950	F	NS
Production overheads	14,190	12,500	F	S
Non-production overheads	16,190	17,880	A	S

117 IVAN LTD

Cost type	Budget £	Actual £	Variance £	Adverse or favourable (A or F)
Sales	544,750	547,450	2,700	F
Direct materials	76,800	80,200	3,400	A
Direct labour	148,400	146,000	2,400	F
Production overheads	136,000	144,200	8,200	A
Administration overheads	105,000	109,800	4,800	A

118 BLUEBELL LTD

Cost type	Budget £	Actual £	Variance £	Adverse/ Favourable	%
Sales	£204,555	£197,455	7,100	A	3
Direct materials	£39,000	£42,300	3,300	A	8
Direct labour	£75,000	£83,000	8,000	A	11
Production overheads	£69,000	£64,800	4,200	F	6
Administration overheads	£53,000	£58,900	5,900	A	11

Section 3

MOCK AND SAMPLE ASSESSMENTS – QUESTIONS

TASK 1 **(8 MARKS)**

(a) Identify the following statements as being true or false by putting a tick in the relevant column of the table below: **(4 marks)**

Statement	True	False
• Labour paid by a simple piecework system is a variable cost.	✓	
• FIFO is a useful inventory valuation method for materials where individual units are not separately identifiable.	✓	✓
• A cost unit is a separately identifiable part of the business where the manager is only responsible for divisional costs.		✓
• Classification of cost by behaviour is particularly useful for budgeting.	✓	

(b) Indicate whether each of the following statements regarding management accounting is true or false by putting a tick in the relevant column of the table below: **(4 marks)**

Characteristic	True	False
• Statements produced by management accounting are primarily for internal use.	✓	
• Management accounting statements are typically used to help identify the organisation's tax liability.		✓
• Management accountants produce the statement of profit or loss (income statement).		✓
• Management accounting statements normally focus on analysing past transactions.		✓

TASK 2 (8 MARKS)

Morden makes and sells postcards.

(a) **Classify the following costs by element (material, labour or overhead) by putting a tick in the relevant column of the table below:** (4 marks)

Cost	Material	Labour	Overheads
• Wages paid to Morden's photographer for pictures used in postcards.		✓	✓
• Ink used to print postcards.	✓		
• Maintenance of printers used to produce postcards.			✓
• Delivery costs to customers.			✓

Mitcham buys large rolls of wire, cuts them into various sizes and sells it on to customers.

(b) **Classify the following costs by nature (direct or indirect) by putting a tick in the relevant column of the table below:** (4 marks)

Cost	Direct	Indirect
• Wages of cutting staff.	✓	
• Depreciation of cutting machinery.		✓
• Wages of the cutting staff supervisor.		✓
• Purchase of rolls of wire.	✓	

TASK 3 (8 MARKS)

Bank is a company that builds houses.

(a) **Classify the following costs by function (production, admin, selling and distribution or finance) by putting a tick in the relevant column of the table below:** (4 marks)

Cost	Production	Admin	Selling and distribution	Finance
• Bank charges.				✓
• Purchase of bricks.	✓			
• Depreciation of office computers.		✓		
• Wages paid to advertising staff.			✓	

(b) **Classify the following costs by behaviour (fixed, variable, semi-variable or stepped) by putting a tick in the relevant column of the table below:** **(4 marks)**

Statement	Fixed	Variable	Semi-variable	Stepped
• Purchase of plots of land to be used for building new houses.	✓	✓	'	
• Hire of digging equipment. One digger is required for every 15 houses built.		✓		✓
• Bank' total wages bill – including salaried workers as well as those paid piecework.		'	✓	
• Rent on Bank's head office building.	✓			

TASK 4   (6 MARKS)

Cesto Plc is a supermarket and uses a coding system for its elements of cost (materials, labour or overheads) and then further classifies each element by nature (direct or indirect cost) as below. So, for example, the code for direct materials is A100.

Element of cost	Code	Nature of cost	Code
Materials	A	Direct	100
		Indirect	200
Labour	B	Direct	100
		Indirect	200
Overheads	C	Direct	100
		Indirect	200

Code the following costs, extracted from invoices and payroll, using the table below:

Cost	Code
• Purchase of milk for resale in Cesto's stores.	A 100
• Wages of shelf-stackers in Cesto's stores.	B 100
• Salaries of Cesto's store managers.	B 200
• Public indemnity insurance.	C 200
• Purchase of cleaning products for resale in Cesto's stores.	A 100
• Supermarket staff canteen wages.	B 200

TASK 5 (6 MARKS)

FFF is a company that manufactures three different types of fizzy drink – A, B and C. It uses an alpha code for the revenue, costs or investments and then further classifies numerically as shown below:

Activity	Code	Nature of cost	Sub-code
Revenues	RE	Drink A	100
		Drink B	200
		Drink C	300
Costs	CO	Material	520
		Labour	620
		Overheads	720
Investments	IV	Drink A	100
		Drink B	200
		Drink C	300

Code the following costs, extracted from invoices and payroll, using the table below. Each transaction should have a five character code.

Cost	Code
• Investment in new machinery to manufacture Drink A.	IV 100
• Wages paid to staff making Drink C.	CO 620
• Sales of Drink C to Cesto Supermarkets.	RE 300
• Purchase of sugar for use in Drinks A and C.	CO 520
• Head office rental.	CO 720
• Investment in new factory for Drink C.	IV 300

TASK 6 (9 MARKS)

(a) Identify the type of cost behaviour (fixed, variable or semi variable) described in each statement by putting a tick in the relevant column of the table below: (3 marks)

Statement	Fixed	Variable	Semi variable
• Costs are £8,000 at 3,000 units and £12,500 at 6,000 units.			✓
• Cost per unit is £5 per unit if 10,000 units are made and £10 per unit if 5,000 units are made.	✓		
• Total cost is £10,000 if 2,500 units are made and £16,000 if 4,000 units are made.		✓	

(b) Complete the table below by inserting all costs for the activity levels of 5,000 and 9,000 units: **(6 marks)**

	5,000 units	6,000 units	7,500 units	9,000 units
Variable cost (£)	8750			15750
Fixed cost (£)	8000			8000
Total cost (£)	16750	18,500	21,125	23750

2112S - 13125 = 8000   7500 - 6000 = 1500   = 2625 = 1·75
                       21125 - 18500 = 2625   1500
                    18500 - (6000 × 1·75) = 8000

TASK 7 **(7 MARKS)**

(a) Identify the following costs are an overhead or not by putting a tick in the relevant column of the table below: **(3 marks)**

Statement	Yes	No
• Depreciation of production machinery.	✓	
• Fees paid for an external health and safety audit of production.	✓	
• Hours paid to workers on a piecework basis.		✓

Jericho Ltd makes a single product and for a production level of 16,000 units has the following cost details:

Materials   8,000 kilos at £5 per kilo   8000 × 5 = 40000

Labour   32,000 hours at £8 an hour   32000 × 8 = 256000

Fixed Overheads   £224,000

(b) Complete the table below to show the unit cost at a REVISED production level of 20,000 units. Work to the nearest penny. **(4 marks)**

Element	Unit cost
Materials	£ 2·5
Labour	£ 16·00
Overheads	£ 11·2
Total	£ 26·70

40000
16000

256000
16000

→ 224000
22000

TASK 8 (8 MARKS)

Jackson Ltd is looking to calculate the unit cost for one of the products it makes. It needs to calculate an overhead absorption rate to apply to each unit. The methods it is considering are a rate per machine hour, a rate per labour hour, and a rate per unit.

Total factory activity is forecast as follows:

Machine hours	36,000
Labour hours	45,000
Units	216,000
Overheads	£540,000

(a) Complete the table below to show the possible overhead absorption rates that Jackson Ltd could use. The absorption rates should be calculated to two decimal places. **(4 marks)**

	Machine hour	Labour hour	Unit
Overheads (£)	540000	540000	540000
Activity	36000	45000	216000
Absorption rate (£)	15	12	2·5

The following data relates to making one unit of the product:

Material	3 kilos at £5 per kilo
Labour	20 minutes at £15 per hour
Production time	15 minutes

(b) Complete the table below (to two decimal places) to calculate the total unit cost, using the three overhead absorption rates you have calculated in (a). **(4 marks)**

Cost	Machine hour (£)	Labour hour (£)	Unit (£)
Material	15	15	15
Labour	5	5	5
Direct cost	20	20	20
Overheads	$\frac{15}{60} \times 15 = 3·75$	$\frac{20}{60} \times 12 = 4$	2·5
Total unit cost	23·75	4	22·5

TASK 9 (15 MARKS)

(a) Reorder the following costs into a manufacturing account format for the year ended 31 June. Use the columns to the right of the table below to enter your answer. (10 marks)

Purchases of raw materials	22,000	OIRM	6000
Direct labour	45,000	PIRM	22000
Opening inventory of finished goods	2,500	CIRM	(6400)
COST OF GOODS SOLD		DMU	21600
Opening inventory of raw materials	6,000	DL	45000
DIRECT MATERIALS USED		DC	66600
Manufacturing overheads	17,000	MO	17000
Opening inventory of work in progress	4,000	MC	836000
Closing inventory of finished goods	4,500	O.IWP	4000
MANUFACTURING COST		C IWP	(2800)
Closing inventory of work in progress	2,800	CoGM	84800
Closing inventory of raw materials	6,400	OIFG	2500
DIRECT COST		CIFG	(4500)
COST OF GOODS MANUFACTURED		CoGS	82800

(b) Enter the correct figures for the following costs which were not provided in part (a)

(5 marks)

Cost	£
DIRECT MATERIALS USED	21600
DIRECT COST	66600
MANUFACTURING COST	836000
COST OF GOODS MANUFACTURED	84800
COST OF GOODS SOLD	82800

[handwritten annotations at top:]
25000 X6 =150000
50000 X3·75 = 187500
60,000 X7 = 420000

FIFO = 150000 + 35000 X 3·75 = 281250 &CI = 56250
ETFO = 187500 + 10000 X6 = 247500 &CI = 90,000
AVCO = 337500 / 75000 = 4·5 X60000 = 270,000 = 67500

TASK 10   (6 MARKS)

Gravy Ltd carries a single type of raw material. At the start of the month, there were 25,000 litres of the material in inventory, valued at £6 per litre. During the month, Gravy bought another 50,000 litres at £3.75 per litre, followed by an issue to production of 60,000 litres at £7 per litre.

(a) **Identify the valuation method described in the statements below by putting a tick in the relevant column.** (3 marks)

Statement	FIFO	LIFO	AVCO
Closing inventory is valued at £67,500.			✓
The issue of inventory is costed at £281,250.	✓		
The issue of inventory is costed at £247,500.		✓	

(b) **Identify whether the statements in the table are true or false by putting a tick in the relevant column.** (3 marks)

[handwritten left margin: LIFO, FIFO ←]

Statement	True	False
• FIFO values closing inventory at £90,000.		✓
• LIFO values closing inventory at £56,250.		✓
• AVCO values the issue of inventory at £270,000.	✓	

TASK 11   (6 MARKS)

Boat Ltd has the following movements in a certain type of stock into and out of it stores for the month of July.

DATE	RECEIPTS		ISSUES	
	Units	Cost	Units	Cost
July 6	350	£6,125	*17·5*	
July 12	500	£8,125	*16·25*	
July 17	150	£2,850	*19*	
July 22	*400-150=250*	*250 X*	400	
July 30	100	£2,000		

Complete the table below for the issue and closing stock values. Enter figures to the nearest penny.

Method	Cost of Issue on 22 July	Closing Stock at 31 July
FIFO *6125+(650 X16·25) =6125+812·5*	£ *6937·50*	£ *1262·5*
LIFO *2850+250X16·25*	£ *2850+4062·50=6912·50*	£ *12187·50*
AVCO *17100/1000 =17·1*	£ *6840*	£ *12260*

[handwritten calculations at bottom:]
8125
4063

2850
4063
6913

6125
8125
2850
2000

19100-6913=12187

- 6913

TASK 12 (9 MARKS)

An employee is paid £5 per unit, and is expected to make 3 units per hour. Any work in excess of this is paid a bonus of £0.50 per unit.

(a) **Identify the following statements as either true or false by putting a tick in the relevant column of the table below:** (3 marks)

Statement	True	False
• During a 31 hour working week, the employee made 92 units and did not receive a bonus.	✓	
• During a 34 hour working week, the employee made 107 units and earned total pay of £537.50.	✓	
• During a 25 hour week, the employee made 74 units and earned a £0.50 bonus.		✓

Daft Ltd pays a time-rate of £15 per hour to its direct labour for a standard 35 hour week. Any of the labour force working in excess of 35 hours is paid an overtime rate of 'time and a half'.

(b) **Calculate the gross wage for the week for the two workers in the table below:** (6 marks)

Worker	Hours worked	Basic wage	Overtime	Gross wage
S. Illy	37 hours	£ 525	£ 22.5 × 2 = 45	£ 570
C. Razy	43 hours	£ 525	£ 22.5 × 8 = 180	£ 705

TASK 13 (4 MARKS)

Identify the following statements regarding labour payments as either true or false by putting a tick in the relevant column.

Statement	True	False
• An employee who is paid piecework could see a rise in their total pay if they work more hours.	✓	
• Fixed salary staff are likely to have a higher focus on quality than staff who are paid piecework.	✓	
• Employees who are paid an hourly rate will earn more if they are more productive.		✓
• Piecework systems enable the company to cut its wages expense if it does not need to make any more units.	✓	

(**TASK 14**)   **(10 MARKS)**

Sharp Ltd has produced a performance report detailing budgeted and actual information for last month.

(a)   **Calculate the amount of the variance for each cost type and enter it into the table below. Determine whether it is adverse or favourable and put an A or F in the relevant column.**

(6 marks)

Cost type	Budget £	Actual £	Variance £	Adverse or Favourable (A or F)
Sales revenue	25,550	26,888	*1338 A	F
Direct labour	16,000	17,512	1512 A	A
Direct materials	2,995	2,875	120 f	F
Administration overheads	2,785	2,875	90	A
Selling and distribution overheads	4,100	4,298	198	A

(b)   **Identify whether the following statements are true or false:**   **(4 marks)**

Statement	True	False
If budgeted sales are 6,000 units at £10.50 per unit, and actual sales are £65,000, the sales variance is adverse	A W	✓
A favourable cost variance occurs when an actual cost of £8,400 is compared to a budgeted cost of £9 per unit for an output of 945 units.	✓	
A variance arises from a comparison of actual costs for last period with budgeted costs for a future period.		✓
If actual labour costs are the same as budgeted labour costs then no variance arises.	✓	

Handwritten margin notes:

Sales Rev
B = 63000
A = 65000

B
= 945×9 = 8505
A = 8400

Actual cost is higer is Adverse
A   "   "   " lower is fav

TASK 15 (10 MARKS)

Shark Ltd has produced a performance report detailing budgeted and actual information for last month.

(a) Calculate the variance for each item and enter the value in the relevant column. Shark considers significant variances to be any in excess of 6% of budget. For the variances calculated, enter S for significant and NS for not significant in the relevant column. Variances should be calculated to two decimal places. **(6 marks)**

Cost type	Budget £	Actual £	Variance £	Significant or Not Significant (S or NS)
Sales revenue	160,000	165,400	5400	NS
Direct labour	45,000	49,500	4500	S
Direct materials	22,700	21,100	1600	S
Administration overheads	6,500	9,255	2755	S
Selling and distribution overheads	25,795	27,105	1310	NS

Handwritten annotations in right margin: 3'38<6, 10%6, 7%6, 42%6, 5<6

(b) Identify whether the following statements are true or false: **(4 marks)**

Statement	True	False
• An adverse Direct Labour cost variance should be reported to the sales manager		✓
• A favourable Direct Material cost variance should be reported to the purchasing manager.	✓	
• A variance considered to be Not Significant should be reported to the Chief Executive.		✓
• If actual labour costs are the same as budgeted labour costs then no variance should be reported.	✓	

SAMPLE ASSESSMENT 1 – QUESTIONS

TASK 1 (8 MARKS)

Costing uses a number of techniques to assist management.

(a) **Identify the following statements as being true or false by putting a tick in the relevant column of the table below.** (4 marks)

Statement	True	False
A positive cost variance means actual costs are less than budgeted costs.	✓	
Wages of production workers are a direct cost.	✓	
Variable costs increase in total as output increases.	✓	
The piecework method for labour payment ensures a set wage each week for employees.		✓

The table below lists some characteristics of financial accounting and management accounting.

(b) **Indicate the characteristics for each system by putting a tick in the relevant column of the table below.** (4 marks)

Characteristic	Financial accounting	Management accounting
The statements of this system are of interest mainly to the managers of a business.		✓
This system uses techniques to cost inventory issues to production.		✓
This system uses techniques to arrive at a unit cost for a product or service.		✓
The statements of this system are used as a basis to calculate the tax liability of a business.	✓	✓

TASK 2 (8 MARKS)

Chippy Ltd is in business as a furniture maker.

(a) **Classify the following costs by behaviour (fixed, variable or semi-variable) by putting a tick in the relevant column of the table below.** (4 marks)

Cost	Variable	Fixed	Semi-variable
Wood purchased for production.	✓		
Wages of carpenters paid on a piecework basis.	✓		
Workshop heating costs consisting of a fixed and usage charge.			✓
Salary of workshop manager.		✓	

Makewell Ltd is in business as a pharmacist, manufacturing and selling drugs.

(b) **Classify the following costs incurred by nature (direct or indirect) by putting a tick in the relevant column of the table below.** (4 marks)

Cost	Direct	Indirect
Insurance of premises.		✓
Salaries of pharmacists who make the drugs.	✓	
Training course for pharmacy assistants.		✓
Drugs purchased for resale.	✓	

TASK 3 (6 MARKS)

Hardcastle Ltd, a steel manufacturer, has set up an investment centre for an investment project it is undertaking over a period of years. It uses an alpha coding system for its investments, revenues and costs, and then classifies them numerically as outlined in the first four columns of the table below.

Activity	Code	Nature of cost	Sub-code
Investments	IVS	External	107
		Internal	109
Revenues	RVS	UK Sales	214
		Rest of World Sales	218
Costs	CVS	Material	435
		Labour	545
		Overheads	675

Code the following transactions for the project, using the table below. Each transaction should have a six character code

Transaction	Code
Iron ore purchased for production.	CVS/435
Wages of steel mill workers.	CVS/545
Repairs to steel-making equipment.	CVS/475
Sales of steel to UK car manufacturers.	RVS/214
Bank loan raised for project.	IMS/107
Sales of steel to South America.	RVS/248

TASK 4 (12 MARKS)

(a) Identify the type of cost behaviour (fixed, variable or semi-variable) described in each statement by putting a tick in the relevant column of the table below. (6 marks)

Cost	Fixed	Variable	Semi-variable
At 9,000 units this cost is £28,000, and at 12,000 units it is £34,000.			✓
At 5,000 units, this cost is £5.20 per unit, and at 8,000 units it is £3.25 per unit.	✓		
At 11,000 units this cost is £49,500, and at 15,000 units it is £67,500.		✓	

Handwritten margin notes: 3·11, 2·83, 26000, 2600, 4·5, 4·5

(b) Complete the table below by inserting all costs for the activity levels of 3,000 and 7,000 units. (6 marks)

Handwritten note above 3,500 column: 1500

	3,000 units	3,500 units	5,000 units	7,000 units
Variable cost (£)	9000			21000
Fixed cost (£)	12000			12000
Total cost (£)	21000	£22,500	£27,000	33000

Handwritten working:

4500

$\dfrac{4500}{1500} = 3$

FC = 22500 − (3500 × 3)
= 22500 − 10500
= 12000

TASK 5 (12 MARKS)

Hardcast Ltd is looking to calculate the unit cost for one of the products it makes. It needs to calculate an overhead absorption rate to apply to each unit. The methods it is considering are:

- per machine hour

- per labour hour

- per unit

Total factory activity is forecast as follows:

Machine hours	20,000
Labour hours	25,000
Units	120,000
Overheads	£300,000

(a) **Complete the table below to show the possible overhead absorption rates that Hardcast Ltd could use. The absorption rates should be calculated to two decimal places. (3 marks)**

	Machine hour	Labour hour	Unit
Overheads (£)	300,000	300,000	300,000
Activity	20,000	25,000	120,000
Absorption rate (£)	15	12	2·5

The following data relates to making one unit of the product:

Material	4 kilos at £5 per kilo
Labour	15 minutes at £20 per hour
Production time	12 minutes

$\frac{15}{60} = \frac{1}{4} \times 20 = 5$

$\frac{12}{60} = \frac{1}{5} \times 15 =$

(b) **Complete the table below (to two decimal places) to calculate the total unit cost, using the three overhead absorption rates you have calculated in (a). (9 marks)**

Cost	Machine hour (£)	Labour hour (£)	Unit (£)
Material	20	20	20
Labour	5	5	5
Direct cost	25	25	25
Overheads	$\frac{12}{60} \times 15 = 3$	$\frac{15}{60} \times 12 = 3$	2·5
Total unit cost	28	28	27·50

$\frac{15}{60} \times 20$

$\frac{12}{60} \times 150$

$\frac{15^3}{60_8} \times 12$

TASK 6 (12 MARKS)

Eastnite's managers wish to know how fixed costs, variable costs, total costs and unit cost behave at different levels of production.

They have informed you that fixed costs are £36,000 and variable costs are £4.50 per unit.

Complete the table below. Unit costs should be calculated to two decimal places.

Units	Fixed costs £	Variable costs £	Total costs £	Unit cost £
4,000	36000	18000	54000	13'5
6,000	36000	27000	63000	10'5
10,000	36000	45000	81000	8'10

TASK 7 (14 MARKS)

(a) Reorder the following costs into a manufacturing account format for the year ended 31 December. Use the columns to the right of the table below to enter your answer.

(9 marks)

DIRECT MATERIALS USED		OIRM	24600
Opening inventory of work in progress	59,000	PORM	66000
Closing inventory of raw materials	43,200	CIRM	(43200)
MANUFACTURING COST		DMU	47400
COST OF GOODS SOLD		DL	89200
DIRECT COST		DC	13660
Closing inventory of finished goods	71,700	MO	129700
Opening inventory of raw materials	24,600	MC	266300
Manufacturing overheads	129,700	OIWIP	59000
Direct labour	89,200	CIWIP	(51600)
COST OF GOODS MANUFACTURED		COGF	273700
Closing inventory of work in progress	51,600	OIFG	73400
Opening inventory of finished goods	73,400	CIFG	(71700)
Purchases of raw materials	66,000	C	275400

(b) Determine and enter the cost totals below, using your answer from part (a) to help you

(5 marks)

DIRECT MATERIALS USED	£	47400
DIRECT COST	£	13660
MANUFACTURING COST	£	266300
COST OF GOODS MANUFACTURED	£	273700
COST OF GOODS SOLD	£	275400

TASK 8 (9 MARKS)

You are told the opening inventory of a single raw material in the stores is 1,800 units at £4.00 per unit. During the month, 2,100 units at £4.10 per unit are received and the following week 2,600 units are issued.

(a) **Identify the valuation method by dragging the statements into the correct column below.**

(6 marks)

FIFO	LIFO	AVCO
5330	10610	5270

Statements: *TP = 7200 + 8610 = 15810*

1800 × 4 = 7200
2100 × 4'10 = 8610
2600 ÷ ?

- The closing inventory is valued at £5,270

- The closing inventory is valued at £5,330   *AVCO = 15810*
  3900
  = 4'05

- he issue of 2,600 units is costed at £10,610   *= 2600 × 4'05*
  = 10540
  CI = 15810 − 10540

FIFo = 7200 + (800 × 4'10)
= 7200 + 3280
= 10480
CI = 15810 − 10480 = 5330

LIFO = 8610 + (500 × 4)
= 8610 + 2000 = 10610
CI = (15810 − 10610)
= 5200

(b) **Identify whether the statements in the table below are true or false.** *= 5270* (3 marks)

Statement	True	False
AVCO costs the issue of 2,600 units at £10,540.	✓	
LIFO values the closing inventory at £5,200.	✓	
FIFO values the closing inventory at £5,200.		✓

TASK 9 (12 MARKS)

A business has the following movements in a certain type of inventory into and out of its stores for the month of September. There was no opening inventory:

DATE	RECEIPTS		ISSUES	
	Units	Cost	Units	Cost
3 September	1,500	£3,000	2	
11 September	1,600	£3,520	2'2	
14 September	1,900	£4,275	2'25	
19 September			4,000	
28 September	1,000	£2,750		

13545

Complete the table below for the issue and closing inventory values.

Method	Cost of issue on September 19 (£)	Closing inventory at September 30 (£)
FIFO *3000 + 3520 + (900×2'2)* *3000 + 3520 + 2025*	8545	5000
LIFO *3520 + 4275 + (500×2)*	8795	4750
AVCO *10795/9000 = 2'16× 4050*	8636	4909

(handwritten margin notes at top: 1 hr = 20 ÷ ... 20 U = 1, 20 U 1 U = 1/20, 900/200 = ... 36 = ... 120 U ... 36×15 = 540 + ... × 15.25 = 540 + 30.5)

TASK 10 (8 MARKS)

An employee is paid £15 per hour and is expected to make 20 units per hour. For any excess production, the employee will be paid a bonus of £0.25 per unit.

(a) **Identify the following statements as being true or false by putting a tick in the relevant column of the table below.** (6 marks)

Statement	True	False
During a 36 hour working week, the employee produces <u>800</u> units and earns total pay of £580.		✓
During a 38 hour week the employee produces 880 units and earns a bonus of £30.	✓	✓
During a 39 hour week the employee produces 1,000 units and earns total pay of £640.	✓	

(handwritten margin left: 38×15 = 570, 760 − 880 = 120 = 120 unit / 20 = 6, 120×0.25 = 30)

Amplefort Ltd pays a time-rate of £13.50 per hour for a 38 hour week. Any employee working in excess of 38 hours per week is paid an overtime rate of £20.50 per hour.

(b) **Calculate the basic wage, overtime and gross wage for the week for the two employees in the table below. Note: If no overtime is paid, you should enter 0 as the overtime for that employee.** (2 marks)

(handwritten margin left: 1 W2 = 20, 39 h ... = 780 ×15.25, = 1000 − 780, = 220 units, 220×0.25 = 655, 220×0.25 = 585, 39×15 = 640, 585+55 = 640)

Worker	Hours worked	Basic wage (£)	Overtime (£)	Gross wage (£)
S Albertini	40	513	2 × 20.50 = 41	554
J Asheef	44	513	6 × 20.50 = 123	636

TASK 11 (8 MARKS)

Elbright Ltd wishes to pay its employees using either the time-rate method with bonus, or the piecework method. The time-rate used is £11.25 per hour and an employee is expected to produce <u>12 units per hour</u>, and anything over this is paid a bonus of £0.60 per unit. The piecework payment rate is £0.90 per unit.

Complete the table below for the two methods, showing the gross wage for the time-rate with bonus and the piecework wage.

Note: If no bonus is paid, you should enter 0 as the bonus for that employee in the table.

Hours worked	Unit output	Basic wage £	Bonus £	Gross wage £	Piecework wage £
40	540	450	60×'6= 36	486	486
44	520	495	8×'0	495	520×0.9 = 468

(handwritten working below table, left column:
40 hr Basic wage = 40 × 11.25
40 h = 40 × ... = 450
40 hr Unit = 40 × 12 = 480
= 540 − 480 = 60 × 0.60 = 36
44 hr Basic wage = 495
44 hr Unit = 44 × 12 = 528
= 520 < 528 = 0 Bonus*)

KAPLAN PUBLISHING

TASK 12 (12 MARKS)

A number of statements about budgeting are set out in the table below

(a) **Identify whether the following statements are true or false by putting a tick in the relevant column of the table below.** (4 marks)

Statement	True	False
If budgeted sales are 5,000 units at £11.50 per unit and actual sales are £59,000, the sales variance is adverse B=57500 f A =59000 f	\	✓
A favourable cost variance occurs when an actual cost of £4,800 is compared to a budgeted cost of £12 per unit for a budgeted output of 395 units A = 4800 AD B = 4740		✓
A variance arises from a comparison of budgeted costs from a past period with budgeted costs of a future period		✓
If actual material costs are the same as budgeted costs for materials then no variance arises	✓	

Martial has produced a performance report detailing budgeted and actual costs for last month

(a) **In the table below, determine whether the variance is adverse or favourable (enter A or F).** (8 marks)

Cost type	Budget £	Actual £	Adverse or favourable (A or F)
Direct material	93,750	93,720	F
Direct labour	74,280	74,240	F
Production overheads	94,650	94,670	A
Administration overheads	46,360	46,275	F
Selling and distribution overheads	69,100	69,180	A

TASK 13 (12 marks)

The manager of Draycott Ltd has requested a performance report detailing budgeted data, actual data and variances for last month.

Budgeted data for the month included:

Sales	6,800 units at £60 per unit	= 408000
Material	5,100 kilos at £25 per kilo	= 127500
Labour	4,850 hours at £30 per hour	= 145500
Overheads	£107,000	

In the table below, insert the budgeted amount for each item, calculate each variance and then determine whether it is adverse or favourable (enter A or F).

Item	Budget £	Actual £	Variance £	A or F
Sales	408000	412,400	4400	F
Material	127500	134,700	7200	A
Labour	145500	142,700	2800	F
Overheads	107000	113,200	6200	A

TASK 14 (6 MARKS)

The managers of Dearlove Ltd require the budget report below for last month to be completed. In particular, they want production cost variances expressed as a percentage of budget.

Actual costs were:

Direct material	£117,200
Direct labour	£124,600
Production overheads	£122,900

Calculate the production cost variances and the variances as a percentage of budget, rounded to two decimal places.

You are not required to show whether the variances are adverse or favourable. Do not insert a minus sign or brackets.

Cost	Budget £	Variance £	Variance %
Direct material	114,000	3200	2.81
Direct labour	119,000	5600	96/.
Production overheads	125,000	2100	21/.

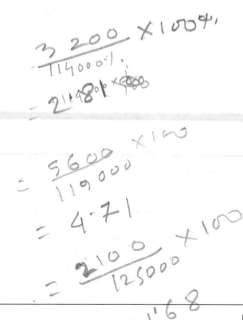

$$\frac{3200}{114000} \times 100\%$$

$$= 2.48\% \times$$

$$= \frac{5600}{119000} \times 100$$

$$= 4.71$$

$$= \frac{2100}{125000} \times 100$$

$$= 1.68$$

TASK 15 (8 MARKS)

Last month's performance report for Francome Ltd is summarised in the table below. Any variance in excess of 10% of budget is deemed to be significant and should be reported to the relevant managers for review and appropriate action.

(a) **Examine the variances in the table and then determine whether they are significant (S) or Not Significant (NS) in the relevant column below.** (4 marks)

Cost	Budget £	Variance £	Significant (S) or Not Significant (NS)
Direct materials Department A	101,200	10,020	NS
Direct materials Department B	98,500	9,700	NS
Direct Labour Department A	97,250	9,740	S
Direct Labour Department B	72,500	7,450	S

(b) **Identify whether the following statements are true or false by putting a tick in the relevant column of the table below.** (4 marks)

Statement	True	False
The variance for the Direct Material cost of Department A should be reported to the purchasing manager		✓
The variance for the Direct Labour cost of Department A should be reported to the production manager for Department B		✓
The variance for the Direct Labour cost of Department B should be reported to the sales manager		✓
The variance for the Direct Material cost of Department B should be reported to the production manager for Department B		✓

SAMPLE ASSESSMENT 2 – QUESTIONS

TASK 1   (8 MARKS)

Costing uses a number of techniques to assist management.

(a) **Identify the following statements as being true or false by putting a tick in the relevant column of the table below.**   **(4 marks)**

Statement	True	False
Manufacturing overheads are a direct manufacturing cost.		✓
The variable cost per unit increases as more units are produced.		✓
Issues of inventory using first in, first out (FIFO) will always be costed at the earliest purchase price.	✓	
An adverse sales variance is where actual sales revenue is less than budgeted sales revenue.	✓	

MO are indirect cost

Rev AↃ Bↁ

The table below lists some of the characteristics of financial accounting and cost accounting.

(b) **Indicate the characteristics for each system by putting a tick in the relevant column of the table below.**   **(4 marks)**

Characteristic	Financial accounting	Cost accounting
The statements of this system are usually only available to the managers of the business.		✓
The statements of this system are used to determine the tax liability of the business.	✓	
The statements of this system are usually prepared from the past transactions of the business.	✓	
The statements of this system are used to estimate the cost of producing a product or providing a service.		✓

TASK 2 (8 MARKS)

Taste Ltd is in business as a restaurant.

(a) **Classify the following costs Taste Ltd incurred by element (material, labour or overhead).**

(4 marks)

Cost	Material	Labour	Overhead
Food for restaurant meals.	✓		
Rent of restaurant.			✓
Wages paid to waiters and waitresses.		✓	
Food hygiene training course for kitchen staff.			✓

Croome Ltd manufactures and sells garden furniture.

(b) **Classify the following costs incurred by their behaviour (fixed, variable or semi-variable.**

(4 marks)

Cost	Fixed	Variable	Semi-variable
Wood used to make garden furniture.		✓	
Annual rent of factory premises.	✓		
Wages paid on the basis of output.		✓	
Electricity, consisting of a standing charge and a charge for each unit of electricity used.			✓

TASK 3 (6 MARKS)

Blackwater Ltd, a boat builder,has et up an investment centre for an investment project it is undertaking over a period of years. It uses an alpha coding system for its investments, revenues and costs, and then classifies them numerically as outlined in the first four columns of the table below.

Activity	Code	Nature of cost	Sub-code
Investments	INV	External	910
		Internal	960
Revenues	REV	UK Sales	220
		Europe Sales	240
Costs	COS	Material	510
		Labour	530
		Overheads	550

Code the following transactions for the project, using the table below. Each transaction should have a six character code

Transaction	Code
Project sales made to Italy, Europe.	
Engines purchased to power the boats.	
Rent of boatyard premises used for the project.	
Bank loan raised for investment in the project.	
Project sales arising in the UK.	
Salaries of project staff.	

TASK 4 (12 MARKS)

(a) Identify the type of cost behaviour (fixed, variable or semi-variable) described in each statement by putting a tick in the relevant column of the table below. (6 marks)

Cost	Fixed	Variable	Semi-variable
At 5,000 units this cost is £12,500, and at 3,750 units it is £9,375.		✓	
At 4,000 units, this cost is £4.00 per unit, and at 2,500 units it is £6.40 per unit.	✓		
At 8,000 units this cost is £31,500, and at 10,000 units it is £37,500.			✓

(b) Complete the table below by inserting all costs for the activity levels of 5,000 and 7,500 units. (6 marks)

	4,000 units	5,000 units	7,500 units	9,000 units
Variable cost (£)		17500	26250	
Fixed cost (£)		7500	7500	
Total cost (£)	21,500	25000	33750	39,000

$$\frac{17500}{5000} = 3.5$$

$$21500 - (4000 \times 3.5)$$

$$21500 - 14000 = 7500$$

TASK 5 (12 MARKS)

Fletcher Ltd is looking to calculate the unit cost for one of the products it makes. It needs to calculate an overhead absorption rate to apply to each unit. The methods it is considering are:

- per machine hour

- per labour hour

- per unit

Total factory activity is forecast as follows:

Machine hours	25,000
Labour hours	12,000
Units	45,000
Overheads	£360,000

(a)   **Complete the table below to show the possible overhead absorption rates that Fletcher Ltd could use. The absorption rates should be calculated to two decimal places.**

(3 marks)

	Machine hour	Labour hour	Unit
Overheads (£)	360000	360000	360000
Activity	25000	12000	45000
Absorption rate (£)	14·4	30	8

The following data relates to making one unit of the product:

Material	1.5 kilos at £5 per kilo
Labour	15 minutes at £18 per hour
Production time	30 minutes

$1.5 \times 5 = 7.5$

$\frac{15}{60} \times 18 = 4.5$

(b)   **Complete the table below (to two decimal places) to calculate the total unit cost, using the three overhead absorption rates you have calculated in (a).**   (9 marks)

Cost	Machine hour (£)	Labour hour (£)	Unit (£)
Material	7·5	7·5	7·5
Labour	4·5	4·5	4·5
Direct cost	12·0	12·0	12·0
Overheads	$\frac{30}{60} \times 19.4 = 7.2$	$\frac{15}{60} \times 30 = 7.5$	8
Total unit cost	19·2	19·5	20

TASK 6 (12 MARKS)

Alm Ltd's managers wish to know how fixed costs, variable costs, total costs and unit cost behave at different levels of production.

They have informed you that fixed costs are £15,000 and variable costs are £4.50 per unit.

Complete the table below. Unit costs should be calculated to two decimal places.

Units	Fixed costs £	Variable costs £	Total costs £	Unit cost £
2,000	15000	9000	24000	12
2,500	15000	11250	26250	10'5
5,000	15000	22500	37500	7'5

TASK 7 (14 MARKS)

(a) Reorder the following costs into a manufacturing account format for the year ended 31 December. Use the columns to the right of the table below to enter your answer.

(9 marks)

COST OF GOODS SOLD		O IRM	14650
Manufacturing overheads	45,310	P RM	75110
Closing inventory of work in progress	19,580	C RM	(13290)
DIRECT MATERIALS USED		DMU	76470
DIRECT COST		D L	54980
Purchases of raw materials	75,110	D C	131450
Opening inventory of work in progress	18,340	M O	45310
Closing inventory of finished goods	27,830	M C	176760
COST OF GOODS MANUFACTURED		O IWPP	18340
MANUFACTURING COST		C IWIR	(19580)
Direct labour	54,980	COGM	175520
Opening inventory of raw materials	14,650	O IFG	25670
Opening inventory of finished goods	25,670	C IFG	(27830)
Closing inventory of raw materials	13,290	C GS	173360

(b) **Determine and enter the cost totals below, using your answer from part (a) to help you**

(5 marks)

DIRECT MATERIALS USED	£	76470
DIRECT COST	£	131450
MANUFACTURING COST	£	176760
COST OF GOODS MANUFACTURED	£	175520
COST OF GOODS SOLD	£	173360

TASK 8 (9 MARKS)

You are told the opening inventory of a single raw material in the stores is 2,250 units at £2.50 per unit. During the month, 1,500 units at £2.75 per unit are received and the following week 1,800 units are issued.

AVCO   2250 × 2.50   5625 = 9750 / 3750 = 2.6
        1500 × 2.75   4125

(a) **Identify the valuation method by dragging the statements into the correct column below.**

1800 = ?

(6 marks)

FIFO	LIFO	AVCO
4500	4875	4680

Statements:

- The issue of 1,800 units is costed at £4,500.

- The issue of 1,800 units is costed at £4,680.

- The closing inventory is valued at £4,875.

LIFO = 4125 + 300 × 2.5
cost of Issue 4875
c INV = 9750 − 4875 = 4875

You are told the opening inventory of a single raw material in the stores is 2,250 units at £2.50 per unit. During the month, 1,500 units at £2.75 per unit are received and the following week 1,800 units are issued.

(b) **Identify whether the statements in the table below are true or false.** **(3 marks)**

Statement	True	False
FIFO values the closing inventory at £5,250.	✓	
LIFO costs the issue of 1,800 units at £4,500.		✓
AVCO values the closing inventory at £5,070.	✓	

FIFO
2250 UM → 5625
1 → 5625
1800 → 5625 × 1800 / 2250
Cost of Issue = 4500
c INV = 9750 − 450 = 5250

TASK 9 (12 MARKS)

A business has the following movements in a certain type of inventory into and out of its stores for the month of September. There was no opening inventory:

DATE	RECEIPTS		ISSUES	
	Units	Cost	Units	Cost
5 September	1,000	£5,000	*5*	
9 September	750	£4,500	*6*	
13 September	500	£4,000	*8*	
20 September			1,200	
25 September	600	£4,500		

TP - 18000

Complete the table below for the issue and closing inventory values.

Method	Cost of issue on September 20 (£)	Closing inventory at September 30 (£)
FIFO *5000 + 200 X 6* *5000 + 1200*	6200	11800
LIFO *4000 + 4200 X5*	8200	9800
AVCO *18000/2250 = 8 X1200*	7200	10800

TASK 10 *LIFE 4000 + 4500 + (4200 - 300 = 700 - 750 = 50 X6)* (8 MARKS)
= 4000 + 4500 - 300 (50 unit extra)

An employee is paid £14 per hour and is expected to make 30 units per hour. For any excess production, the employee will be paid a bonus of £0.50 per unit.

(a) **Identify the following statements as being true or false by putting a tick in the relevant column of the table below.** (6 marks)

Statement	True	False
During a 30 hour working week, the employee produces 870 units and earns total pay of £435. *less unit produces so bonus '0"*	*(crossed)*	✓
During a 36 hour week the employee produces 1,100 units and earns a bonus of £10.	✓	
During a 42 hour week the employee produces 1,300 units and earns total pay of £608.	✓	

Pendle Ltd pays a time-rate of £13.50 per hour for a 34 hour week. Any employee working in excess of 34 hours per week is paid an overtime rate of £20.50 per hour.

30×30
=900 -870
= 30
36×195
=504
36×
36×30=1080
1080 -1100 =
=20

£14 per hour
30 unit per hours
bonus = 0'50 per unit
42 X 3 0U= 1260
42 +148 = 588

(b) Calculate the basic wage, overtime and gross wage for the week for the two employees in the table below. Note: If no overtime is paid, you should enter 0 as the overtime for that employee. **(2 marks)**

Worker	Hours worked	Basic wage (£)	Overtime (£)	Gross wage (£)
S Hewitt 1140 unit 38	38	659	4 X 20'50 = 82	541
J Lal 1260	42	889	8 X 20'50 = 164	623

TASK 11 (8 MARKS)

Edwards Ltd wishes to pay its employees using either the time-rate method with bonus, or the piecework method. The time-rate used is £12.50 per hour and an employee is expected to produce 12 units per hour, and anything over this is paid a bonus of £0.50 per unit. The piecework payment rate is £1.10 per unit.

Complete the table below for the two methods, showing the gross wage for the time-rate with bonus and the piecework wage.

Note: If no bonus is paid, you should enter 0 as the bonus for that employee in the table.

Hours worked	Unit output	Basic wage £	Bonus £	Gross wage £	Piecework wage £
34X12=408 — 400	400	425	work less 50	425	440
42 X12 =504 — 530	530	525	13	538	583

TASK 12 (9 marks)

A number of statements about budgeting are set out in the table below

(a) Identify whether the following statements are true or false by putting a tick in the relevant column of the table below. **(4 marks)**

Statement	True	False
A favourable cost variance occurs when an actual cost of £6,500 is compared to a budgeted cost of £11 per unit for a budgeted output of 550 units 6050 B		✓
An adverse cost variance occurs when an actual costs are lower than budgeted costs		✓
A budgeted cost is a forecast cost for a future period	✓	
When budgeted sales revenue is lower than actual sales revenue, there is a favourable sales variance	✓	✗

Onslow Ltd. has produced a performance report detailing budgeted and actual costs for last month

(b)   In the table below, determine whether the variance is adverse or favourable (enter A or F).   (5 marks)

Cost type	Budget £	Actual £	Adverse or favourable (A or F)
Direct material	54,250	53,750	F
Direct labour	33,680	35,120	A
Production overheads	27,950	28,100	A
Administration overheads	15,210	14,980	F
Selling and distribution overheads	13,350	13,690	A

TASK 13   (8 MARKS)

The manager of Khan Ltd has requested a performance report detailing budgeted data, actual data and variances for last month.

Budgeted data for the month included:

Sales	21,200 units at £15 per unit
Material	7,460 kilos at £12 per kilo
Labour	3,210 hours at £11.50 per hour
Overheads	£55,420

In the table below, insert the budgeted amount for each item, calculate each variance and then determine whether it is adverse or favourable (enter A or F).

Item	Budget £	Actual £	Variance £	A or F
Sales	318 000	325,000	7000	F
Material	89520	86,760	2760	F
Labour	36915	37,650	735	A
Overheads	55420	54,690	730	F

TASK 14 (6 MARKS)

The managers of Mistri Ltd require the budget report below for last month to be completed. In particular, they want production cost variances expressed as a percentage of budget.

Actual costs were:

Direct material	£51,400
Direct labour	£44,350
Production overheads	£35,610

Calculate the production cost variances and the variances as a percentage of budget, rounded to two decimal places.

You are not required to show whether the variances are adverse or favourable. Do not insert a minus sign or brackets.

Cost	Budget £	Variance £	Variance %
Direct material	48,500	2900	8·98
Direct labour	45,600	1250	2·74
Production overheads	37,000	1390	3·76

TASK 15 (8 MARKS)

Last month's performance report for Mithian Ltd is summarised in the table below. Any variance in excess of 3% of budget is deemed to be significant and should be reported to the relevant managers for review and appropriate action.

(a) **Examine the variances in the table and then determine whether they are significant (S) or Not Significant (NS) in the relevant column below.** (4 marks)

Cost	Budget £	Variance £	Significant (S) or Not Significant (NS)
Direct materials Department A	53,680	3,120	S
Direct materials Department B	25,310	445	NS
Direct Labour Department A	35,080	2,190	S
Direct Labour Department B	27,860	510	NS

(b) **Identify whether the following statements are true or false by putting a tick in the relevant column of the table below.** **(4 marks)**

Statement	True	False
The variance for the Direct Material cost of Department A should be reported to the Production manager for Department A	✓	
The variance for the Direct Material cost of Department B should be reported to the Purchasing Manager		✓
The variance for the Direct Labour cost of Department B should be reported to the Production Manager for Department B		✓
The variance for the Direct Labour cost of Department A should be reported to the Human Resources Manager	✓	

Section 4

MOCK AND SAMPLE ASSESSMENTS – ANSWERS

TASK 1

(a)

- True
- False
- False
- True

(b)

- True
- False
- False
- False

TASK 2

(a)

- Labour
- Material
- Overheads
- Overheads

(b)

- Direct
- Indirect
- Indirect
- Direct

TASK 3

(a)

- Finance
- Production
- Admin
- Selling and distribution

(b)

- Variable
- Stepped
- Semi-variable
- Fixed

TASK 4

- A100
- B100
- B200
- C200
- A100
- B200

TASK 5

- IV100
- CO620
- RE300
- CO520
- CO720
- IV300

TASK 6

(a)

- Semi variable
- Fixed
- Variable

(b)

	5,000 units	6,000 units	7,500 units	9,000 units
Variable cost (£)	8,750			15,750
Fixed cost (£)	8,000			8,000
Total cost (£)	16,750	18,500	21,125	23,750

Difference in units given = (7,500 – 6,000) = 1,500 units

Difference in total costs given = £21,125 – £18,500 = £2,625

Therefore variable cost per unit = £2,625 ÷ 1,500 = £1.75

At 6,000 units, fixed costs are therefore £18,500 – (6,000 × £1.75) = £8,000

TASK 7

(a)

- Yes
- Yes
- No

(b)

Element	Unit cost
Materials	£2.50
Labour	£16.00
Overheads	£11.20
Total	£29.70

TASK 8

(a)

	Machine hour	Lab
Overheads (£)	540,000	54(
Activity	36,000	45,
Absorption rate (£)	15.00	

126

(b)

Cost	Machine hour (£)	Labour hour (£)	Unit (£)
Material	15.00	15.00	15.00
Labour	5.00	5.00	5.00
Direct cost	20.00	20.00	20.00
Overheads	3.75	4.00	2.50
Total unit cost	23.75	24.00	22.50

TASK 9

(a)

Opening inventory of raw materials	6,000
Purchases of raw materials	22,000
Closing inventory of raw materials	6,400
DIRECT MATERIALS USED	
Direct labour	45,000
DIRECT COST	
Manufacturing overheads	17,000
MANUFACTURING COST	
Opening inventory of work in progress	4,000
Closing inventory of work in progress	2,800
COST OF GOODS MANUFACTURED	
Opening inventory of finished goods	2,500
Closing inventory of finished goods	4,500
COST OF GOODS SOLD	

(b)

Cost	£
DIRECT MATERIALS USED	21,600
DIRECT COST	66,600
MANUFACTURING COST	83,600
COST OF GOODS MANUFACTURED	84,800
COST OF GOODS SOLD	82,800

TASK 10

(a)

- AVCO
- FIFO
- LIFO

(b)

- False
- False
- True

TASK 11

Method	Cost of issue on 22 July	Closing stock at 31 July
FIFO	£6,937.50	£12,162.50
LIFO	£6,912.50	£12,187.50
AVCO	£6,840.00	£12,260.00

TASK 12

(a)

- True
- True
- False

(b)

Worker	Hours worked	Basic wage	Overtime	Gross wage
S. Illy	37 hours	£525	£45	£570
C. Razy	43 hours	£525	£180	£705

TASK 13

- True
- True
- False
- True

TASK 14

(a)

Cost type	Budget £	Actual £	Variance £	Adverse or favourable (A or F)
Sales revenue	25,550	26,888	£1,338	F
Direct labour	16,000	17,512	£1,512	A
Direct materials	2,995	2,875	£120	F
Administration overheads	2,785	2,875	£90	A
Selling and distribution overheads	4,100	4,298	£198	A

(b)

- False
- True
- False
- True

TASK 15

(a)

Cost type	Budget £	Actual £	Variance £	Significant or Not Significant (S or NS)
Sales revenue	160,000	165,400	5,400	NS
Direct labour	45,000	49,500	4,500	S
Direct materials	22,700	21,100	1,600	S
Administration overheads	6,500	9,255	2,755	S
Selling and distribution overheads	25,795	27,105	1,310	NS

(b)

- False
- True
- False
- True

SAMPLE ASSESSMENT 1 ANSWERS

TASK 1 (a)

- True
- True
- True
- False

TASK 1 (b)

- Cost accounting
- Cost accounting
- Cost accounting
- Financial accounting

TASK 2 (a)

- Variable
- Variable
- Semi-variable
- Fixed

TASK 2 (b)

- Indirect
- Direct
- Indirect
- Direct

TASK 3

- CTS435
- CTS545
- CTS675
- RVS214
- IVS107
- RVS218

TASK 4 (a)

- Semi-variable
- Fixed
- Variable

TASK 4 (b)

	3,000 units	3,500 units	5,000 units	7,000 units
Variable cost (£)	9,000			21,000
Fixed cost (£)	12,000			12,000
Total cost (£)	21,000	22,500	27,000	33,000

Using the high-low method, the variable cost per unit and the fixed costs can be calculated as follows:

	Units	Total cost £
High	5,000	27,000
Low	3,500	22,500
Difference	1,500	4,500

The variable cost per unit is therefore £4,500 ÷ 1,500 units = £3

For 3,500 units, total variable cost is therefore (3,500 × £3) £10,500

Fixed costs are therefore (£22,500 − £10,500) £12,000

TASK 5 (a)

	Machine hour	Labour hour	Unit
Overheads (£)	300,000	300,000	300,000
Activity	20,000	25,000	120,000
Absorption rate (£)	15.00	12.00	2.50

TASK 5 (b)

Cost	Machine hour (£)	Labour hour (£)	Unit (£)
Material	20.00	20.00	20.00
Labour	5.00	5.00	5.00
Direct cost	25.00	25.00	25.00
Overheads	3.00	3.00	2.50
Total unit cost	28.00	28.00	27.50

TASK 6

Units	Fixed costs £	Variable costs £	Total costs £	Unit cost £
4,000	36,000	18,000	54,000	13.50
6,000	36,000	27,000	63,000	10.50
10,000	36,000	45,000	81,000	8.10

TASK 7 (a)

Opening inventory of raw materials	24,600
Purchases of raw materials	66,000
Closing inventory of raw materials	43,200
DIRECT MATERIALS USED	
Direct labour	89,200
DIRECT COST	
Manufacturing overheads	129,700
MANUFACTURING COST	
Opening inventory of work in progress	59,000
Closing inventory of work in progress	51,600
COST OF GOODS MANUFACTURED	
Opening inventory of finished goods	73,400
Closing inventory of finished goods	71,700
COST OF GOODS SOLD	

TASK 7 (b)

DIRECT MATERIALS USED	£	47,400
DIRECT COST	£	136,600
MANUFACTURING COST	£	266,300
COST OF GOODS MANUFACTURED	£	273,700
COST OF GOODS SOLD	£	275,400

TASK 8 (a)

FIFO	LIFO	AVCO
The closing inventory is valued at £5,330	The issue of 2,600 units is costed at £10,610	The closing inventory is valued at £5,270

TASK 8 (b)

- True
- True
- False

TASK 9

Method	Cost of issue on September 19 (£)	Closing inventory at September 30 (£)
FIFO	8,545	5,000
LIFO	8,795	4,750
AVCO	8,636	4,909

TASK 10 (a)

- False
- True
- True

TASK 10 (b)

Worker	Hours worked	Basic wage £	Overtime £	Gross wage £
S Albertini	40	513	41	554
J Asheet	44	513	123	636

TASK 11

Hours worked	Unit output	Basic wage £	Bonus £	Gross wage £	Piecework wage £
40	540	450	36	486	486
44	520	495	0	495	468

TASK 12 (a)

- False
- False
- False
- True

TASK 12 (b)

Cost type	Budget £	Actual £	Adverse or favourable (A or F)
Direct materials	93,750	93,720	F
Direct labour	74,280	74,240	F
Production overheads	94,650	94,670	A
Administration overheads	46,360	46,275	F
Selling and distribution overheads	69,100	69,180	A

TASK 13

Item	Budget £	Actual £	Variance £	A or F
Sales	408,000	412,400	4,400	F
Material	127,500	134,700	7,200	A
Labour	145,500	142,700	2,800	F
Overheads	107,000	113,200	6,200	A

TASK 14

Cost	Budget £	Variance £	Variance %
Direct material	114,000	3,200	2.81
Direct labour	119,000	5,600	4.71
Production overheads	125,000	2,100	1.68

TASK 15 (a)

- NS
- NS
- S
- S

TASK 15 (b)

- False
- False
- False
- False

SAMPLE ASSESSMENT 2 ANSWERS

TASK 1 (a)

- False
- False
- True
- True

TASK 1 (b)

- Cost accounting
- Financial accounting
- Financial accounting
- Cost accounting

TASK 2 (a)

- Material
- Overhead
- Labour
- Overhead

TASK 2 (b)

- Variable
- Fixed
- Variable
- Semi-variable

TASK 3

- REV/240
- COS/510
- COS/550
- INV/910
- REV/220
- COS/530

TASK 4 (a)

- Variable

- Fixed

- Semi-variable

TASK 4 (b)

	4,000 units	5,000 units	7,500 units	9,000 units
Variable cost (£)		17,500	26,250	
Fixed cost (£)		7,500	7,500	
Total cost (£)	21,500	25,000	33,750	39,000

Using the high-low method, the variable cost per unit and the fixed costs can be calculated as follows:

	Units	Total cost £
High	9,000	39,000
Low	4,000	21,500
Difference	5,000	17,500

The variable cost per unit is therefore £17,500 ÷ 5,000 units = £3.50

For 5,000 units, total variable cost is therefore (5,000 × £3.50) £17,500

Fixed costs are therefore (£25,000 – £17,500) £7,500

TASK 5 (a)

	Machine hour	Labour hour	Unit
Overheads (£)	360,000	360,000	360,000
Activity	25,000	12,000	45,000
Absorption rate (£)	14.40	30.00	8.00

TASK 5 (b)

Cost	Machine hour (£)	Labour hour (£)	Unit (£)
Material	7.50	7.50	7.50
Labour	4.50	4.50	4.50
Direct cost	12.00	12.00	12.00
Overheads	7.20	7.50	8.00
Total unit cost	19.20	19.50	20.00

TASK 6

Units	Fixed costs £	Variable costs £	Total costs £	Unit cost £
2,000	15,000	9,000	24,000	12.00
2,500	15,000	11,250	26,250	10.50
5,000	15,000	22,500	37,500	7.50

TASK 7 (a)

Opening inventory of raw materials	14,650
Purchases of raw materials	75,110
Closing inventory of raw materials	13,290
DIRECT MATERIALS USED	
Direct labour	54,980
DIRECT COST	
Manufacturing overheads	45,310
MANUFACTURING COST	
Opening inventory of work in progress	18,340
Closing inventory of work in progress	19,580
COST OF GOODS MANUFACTURED	
Opening inventory of finished goods	25,670
Closing inventory of finished goods	27,830
COST OF GOODS SOLD	

TASK 7 (b)

DIRECT MATERIALS USED	£	76,470
DIRECT COST	£	131,450
MANUFACTURING COST	£	176,760
COST OF GOODS MANUFACTURED	£	175,520
COST OF GOODS SOLD	£	173,360

TASK 8 (a)

FIFO	LIFO	AVCO
The issue of 1,800 units is costed at £4,500	The closing inventory is valued at £4,875	The issue of 1,800 units is costed at £4,680

TASK 8 (b)

- True
- False
- True

TASK 9

Method	Cost of issue on September 20 (£)	Closing inventory at September 30 (£)
FIFO	6,200	11,800
LIFO	8,200	9,800
AVCO	7,200	10,800

TASK 10 (a)

- False
- True
- True

TASK 10 (b)

Worker	Hours worked	Basic wage £	Overtime £	Gross wage £
S Hewitt	38	459	82	541
J Lal	42	459	164	623

TASK 11

Hours worked	Unit output	Basic wage £	Bonus £	Gross wage £	Piecework wage £
34	400	425	0	425	440
42	530	525	13	538	583

TASK 12 (a)

- False
- False
- True
- True

TASK 12 (b)

Cost type	Budget £	Actual £	Adverse or favourable (A or F)
Direct materials	54,250	53,750	F
Direct labour	33,680	35,120	A
Production overheads	27,950	28,100	A
Administration overheads	15,210	14,980	F
Selling and distribution overheads	13,350	13,690	A

TASK 13

Item	Budget £	Actual £	Variance £	A or F
Sales	318,000	325,000	7,000	F
Material	89,520	86,760	2,760	F
Labour	36,915	37,650	735	A
Overheads	55,420	54,690	730	F

TASK 14

Cost	Budget £	Variance £	Variance %
Direct material	48,500	2,900	5.98
Direct labour	45,600	1,250	2.74
Production overheads	37,000	1,390	3.76

TASK 15 (a)

- S
- NS
- S
- NS

TASK 15 (b)

- True
- False
- False
- True